The
Real
Answer
to
Addiction

The Real Answer to Addiction

Chris Dew

WESTBOW
PRESS®
A DIVISION OF THOMAS NELSON
& ZONDERVAN

WestBow Press books may be ordered through booksellers or by contacting:

WestBow Press
A Division of Thomas Nelson & Zondervan
1663 Liberty Drive
Bloomington, IN 47403
www.westbowpress.com
844-714-3454

ISBN: 978-1-6642-0138-5 (sc)
ISBN: 978-1-6642-0139-2 (hc)
ISBN: 978-1-6642-0137-8 (e)

Library of Congress Control Number: 2020914837

Printed in the United States of America.

WestBow Press rev. date: 08/28/2020

"You are holding a treasure in your hands right now. Treat it as such. Read it, then pass it along to someone else who needs it. Buy a box and keep them with you to hand out to those you come in contact with, because everyone you meet has wrestled with their own addiction or they love someone who has. This book is a gift to our world, and so is Chris Dew."

—Clayton King, author, speaker, teaching pastor at NewSpring Church, founder of Crossroads Camps and Missions

"There's not a better person to learn from if you're trying to fight loneliness, insecurity, anxiety, depression, and addiction than Chris Dew. All of these are symptoms of a deeper joy-robbing root, and in *The Real Answer to Addiction,* Chris shows us the secret to pulling your pain up by the root and getting rid of it for good. Chris's story of battling with addiction and finding true, sustaining fulfillment is one of the most inspiring I've ever heard. This is a must read no matter where you currently find yourself in the fight."

—Davey Blackburn, speaker, author of *Nothing Is Wasted,* host of the *Nothing Is Wasted* podcast, founder of Nothing Is Wasted Ministries

"Chris Dew offers a much-needed perspective on the problem of addiction while pointing to the solution of greater joy only God can give. Read this book and find true hope."

—Sam Rainer, lead pastor of West Bradenton Baptist Church, cohost of the *Est. Church podcast*, president of Church Answers, co-owner of Rainer Publishing, president of Revitalize Network

"Our world is scrambling to find a real solution to the problem of addiction. Chris's experience and real testimony of how to overcome is going to give you hope."

—Brad Cooper, lead pastor of NewSpring Church in Anderson, South Carolina

"Having walked with Chris through various phases of his recovery, I can attest to the significance and validation of his story. You will be blessed and inspired as you get to know him through these pages and as you have personal encounters with him."

—Randy Hiatt, licensed professional counselor and family therapist

"Chris Dew is living, breathing evidence of an empty tomb, and his radical transformation is a testimony to the resurrection power of Jesus Christ. Today, he stands on the precipice of eternity, laboring with all of his might to rescue others from the very death that almost destroyed him. If you long to help others find total joy and satisfaction in Christ, then this book is for you."

—Taylor Burgess, lead pastor of Cross Community Church in Beaufort, South Carolina

"Lots of addicts find sobriety, but very few find freedom and joy. Chris's story is one of freedom, and his insights point the way with such clarity that it puts that freedom within reach of anyone who dares to read on."

—Chris Figaretti, lead pastor of Vineyard Church in Wheeling, West Virginia

"Chris Dew has written a must-read primer for anyone struggling with addiction. Let his pain become your wisdom!"

—Bradley Saxon, founder and president of the Bridge Center Recovery in Anderson, South Carolina

"I have had the joy of journeying with Chris Dew for years now, and it has been an absolute joy to see God plant a dream, watch him water it faithfully, and see the truly beautiful ministry that is now growing rapidly. Freedom and healing aren't just the messages he brilliantly communicates; they are major themes of the life the he has bravely lived."

—Dan Lian, traveling gospel ninja from Melbourne, Australia, and teaching pastor at NewSpring Church

"Chris Dew has a way of connecting with his reader not just because of the incredible content but because he writes from a place of experience and breakthrough! God has been on full display in Chris's life as He has delivered Chris from addiction and now has given him voice to speak life, hope and joy into dark places."

—Dustin McClain, lead pastor of Purpose Church in Murray, Kentucky

"Chris is one of the most passionate people I know. His book is a wise counsel to anyone who needs to have their eyes opened to a brighter future and wants to walk in freedom."

—Christian Knorr, lead pastor of Credo Church in Wuppertal, Germany

CONTENTS

FOREWORD

Addiction looks like the devil. At least to me it does.

I can testify to the destructive power of the darkness of addiction because I've had a front row seat and a backstage pass. In nearly thirty-five years of ministry, I've watched it tear through a man's body and burn through a woman's soul. I've seen its effects spread like the plague through an extended family, and I've watched mothers sob as they drop their children off at detox or visit them in rehab.

But there's another view of addiction, and unfortunately it doesn't get as much coverage. It's the stories that are marked by hope. It's the lives that experience victory over the downward spiral. It's the breathtaking beauty of watching a family find restoration when Mom celebrates a year of sobriety or Dad brings home his first paycheck after landing his first job upon completion of recovery. We need to hear and see more of these stories.

It's seeing someone trade in the label of "addict" for their true identity as a daughter or a son of the Living God.

And that is why I want you—I implore you—to read this book. Chris Dew is a living testimony of the legitimate power of Jesus Christ to bring life where there was once only death. He is exhibit A, a tangible proof that it is possible to be reborn by the gospel.

Chris is my brother and my friend. He was trained for a year in our Crossroads Coaching Network and immediately put into practice everything he learned. We are part of the same church family, and I've seen the Holy Spirit use Chris in our recovery ministry at NewSpring in ways that are hard to even explain. I love his heart for the kingdom of God, and I trust his testimony because I have seen God use it to break heavy chains from the lives of those who thought the ship had sailed, they were damaged goods, and it was too late for them to ever change.

Chris has a testimony that reads like a Hollywood script—the kind they turn into a movie. Yet better than a Hollywood happy ending, Chris's story lands in your heart with the weight of something real—not nostalgia and not anecdotal slogans but hard-fought victory in the daily grind of life as an evangelist, a husband, and a leader who is seeing real-life change all around him in the lives God uses him to touch.

There is one word that makes Chris unique, and it's the thing that draws me to him as a brother: *joy.* The darkness and emptiness and sickness and death have all been replaced with pure joy. It is a joy that has been filtered through the fires of addiction and loss. It has been purified through pain. And now Chris Dew stands on the other side of the enemy's plot to take his life with a story to tell. Like the apostle Paul, Chris bears, on his body, the marks of Christ. He has been touched by the cross of Jesus. His scars tell the story of battles fought and wars won by the grace of God.

I have close friends and family members who are still wrestling the demons of addiction, shame, and regret. And of all the resources I can put in their hands, and the hands of the people who love them and don't know how to help them, this stands at the top. It's why you should read this book. It will help you know what it feels like to be lost, dead on the inside, and in the clutches of the darkness of addiction. It will give you ways to love someone who cannot seem to win. It offers encouragement when you face a setback and hope when you don't know what to do next.

Chris is gifted by God. He is called by God. He's a tremendous communicator and a spellbinding storyteller. And as far as anointed evangelists go, there is no one I trust more with preaching the good news and calling people to make a decision to follow Jesus as Lord and Savior.

You are holding a treasure in your hands right now. Treat it as such. Read it, then pass it along to someone else who needs it. Buy a box and keep them with you to hand out to those you come in contact with, because everyone you meet has wrestled with their own addiction or they love someone who has. This book is a gift to our world, and so is Chris Dew.

Clayton King
Teaching pastor, NewSpring Church, founder of Crossroads Camps and Missions

CHAPTER 1

The Epidemic of Emptiness

"**Y**ou're such a junkie!"

I left the bedroom and sat down on the cold, red, leather couch after yet another violent fight between two starving heroin addicts. We had been living together since my dad passed away eighteen months prior. She was a normal young adult when we met, but my heroin addiction had taken her captive. She was now a shell of a human being, who was working at a strip club to support her habit.

Thud. I was abruptly brought back to my senses. I knew that sound. My dark heart sank to my toes as I stumbled into the other room. She was lying awkwardly on the floor, turning a pale blue color no drug addict ever wants to see.

"Wake up! Wake up! *Wake up!*" I shook her violently. Her lifeless lips pressed against mine as I gave her CPR. *Breath. Breath.* Nothing.

As I called 911, I realized red and blue lights were going to be outside our first-floor apartment in only a matter of minutes. We lived on the "right side of the tracks" in North Raleigh, but we were clearly from the "wrong side of the tracks" as evidenced by our scarred, malnourished arms. The apartment was littered with needles, spoons, baggies, bongs, and all sorts of drug paraphernalia. I grabbed a giant, black trash bag, more alert than I had been in months; frantically filled it; and tossed it over the porch into the darkness. The dispatcher was still asking too many questions, and the girl still lay eerily lifeless.

"God, if You're real, save her, and I will never do drugs again."

There was an urgent knock at the door, and nearly a half dozen EMTs entered our drug lair. They put her on a stretcher, and I followed them to the hospital.

I sat anxiously in the waiting room. *Did she die? Should I leave? What's going to happen to me? Will I go to jail?*

The doctor finally emerged from the double doors. "She woke up" is all I heard before my mind shifted to the four bags of heroin I had left hidden in our lockbox as I was trashing the rest of the paraphernalia.

I raced out of the hospital doors and sped home to fill my disfigured vein and my empty soul with yet another shot of dope.

Are You Like Me?

This is a small window into the emptiness and chaos of my life until 2010. I, like millions of others, was a drug addict. I lived solely to fill the gaping hole in my soul with anything I could get my hands on. Heroin was the only thing that seemed to work—at least for a season.

If you are currently struggling with addiction and can relate to my seemingly hopeless condition, you know the pain of waking up every day desperately empty, trying your hardest to just do the right thing and not use–only to find yourself caving in yet again. You've most likely burned bridges with your parents, friends, and maybe even your spouse or kids. Depending on your specific love drug, you may have severe health and legal issues. You probably can't stand not to be high or drunk, even for a few hours. You just can't stand to be in your own skin. Due to your hopeless condition, I bet suicide has even crept into your mind as an appealing way of escape. All pathways from here look dark and hopeless.

The purpose of this book is to give you hope—to tell you my story of real-life change—as well as to give you the tools to experience a metamorphosis of your own. It most likely won't be easy, but it is worth it! My hope over the next hundred pages or so is to not only provide you with the pathway to real freedom from drug addiction but also to show you the answer to the underlying emptiness that is our real problem. Whatever your situation, there is hope. Whether you're a mom who's lost her kids, currently sitting in a jail cell, or a functional addict trying to keep it hidden, there is hope. Whether you've been to twenty-five treatment centers or you've never really tried to get sober, there is hope. Whether you're homeless or wealthy; black or white; or on alcohol or crack, meth, or heroin, there is hope. Freedom is possible.

The Growing Problem of Addiction

The problem of addiction is on the rise all over the world. More than 60,000 people die each year from drug overdoses in the United States, which is up from 20,000 just a few years ago.[1] More than 19 million American adults are currently battling a substance abuse disorder. That's about one out of every six people. Around 65% of all people in an American prison or jail are there for a charge related to addiction. Addiction costs the United States

---

[1] "Overdose Death Rates," National Institute on Drug Abuse, National Institute of Health, last modified March 10, 2020, https://www.drugabuse.gov/related-topics/trends-statistics/overdose-death-rates.

$200 billion each year. All of these numbers are the highest ever recorded.[2] We are in the middle of an epidemic.

Possibly the most difficult aspect of addiction is the limitation of current methods to provide real help that leads to real freedom. We seek treatment while hoping this will be the last time we'll ever have to endure this painful process, but a few weeks later, we return to our old ways, hurting everyone in our path. We have a genuine desire to change our ways, but nothing seems to work.

The leading methods of treating addiction have often been found lacking by continual relapse and the failure to treat the real issue. I tried most of the popular treatment methods. I committed myself to mental hospitals, starting at age sixteen. I was prescribed dozens of different medications (antidepressants, anti-anxiety medications, opiate blockers, methadone, Suboxone, antipsychotics, and blood pressure medications, just to name a few), with differing results; none was sufficient. I ended up selling most of them to get more of the good stuff. I sat through dozens of counseling sessions. I went to multiple treatment centers. I went to twelve-step meetings. I met with religious and secular addiction professionals. I was put in court-mandated addiction classes. None of it worked for me.

There are not many quality statistics with hard data out there that show the effectiveness of the leading treatment methods, but even the most optimistic statistics report a relapse rate of 40 to 60 percent.[2] From my experience and that of thousands of people I've met all over the world, the "success" stories are few and far between.

Can you relate?

---

[2] "Alcohol and Drug Abuse Statistics," American Addiction Centers, last updated June 1, 2020, https://americanaddictioncenters.org/rehab-guide/addiction-statistics/.

The Real Underlying Issue

What if addiction isn't the main issue but is instead a fruit of a problematic root? Addiction may have the most direct connection to the legal issues, health issues, broken relationships, and the rest of the chaos and destruction of our lives, but what if it's not the original cause? What if it's the branch that holds the dead fruit but the cause lies still deeper at the roots? I started to realize this when I would emerge from twenty-eight days of rehab, after the physical withdrawal and craving had ceased with a strong resolve to not use drugs again. I'd endure a few hours of the "normal life" but would soon feel like I had before I started using drugs. The mundane life mixed with the dreaded emptiness was the perfect environment for my mind to begin swirling with the possibilities of getting high again. I could not handle my internal state and would return to my vomit. What if the real problem is not addiction but the internal emptiness you and I both know so well?

I don't think this problem is limited to drug addicts. Everyone experiences this. We are like kids on Christmas morning who've spent months dreaming about the presents we will find under the tree. We've searched tirelessly through magazines from every store in town to find just the right presents that will make us truly happy. We've made our lists, been good for Santa Claus, and left cookies and milk downstairs, and then finally the day arrives! We run downstairs with great anticipation, tear through all the presents, but still something is missing. Whether we got everything we asked for or a mere lump of coal, we always have the same thought. *This is it? There's got to be something else.* The longing is still there. Why is that?

This is also seen in the evading hope for the next season. As a young child, you can't wait to be a big girl or boy and start going to elementary school. Once you arrive, you realize the dullness of grade school and begin to hope for middle school. *When I get to middle school, there will be kids from other schools and pretty girls, and then I'll be happy.* You arrive at middle school only to find more of the same, and you begin dreaming about the freedom of high school. The same mediocrity reigns in high school, and you begin to dream of moving out of your parents' house. Once you get to college, you realize yet again you still haven't found what you're looking for. Spouses and houses begin to swirl in your mind as the answer to your problem, but with those things come more trials and still more emptiness. Then parenthood, retirement, empty nesting, loss of a spouse, and eventually death—still empty and looking for what will fill our void. Always searching, never finding. Why are we never satisfied with where we currently are?

Future hall of fame quarterback Tom Brady was once asked how he felt to have finally arrived. He had just won his third Super Bowl, is married to a bikini model, and is one of the most recognized athletes of all time. He has more money, houses, cars, and possessions than I would ever know what to do with. *Why is it that I have everything I could ever want and still feel like there's something more?*

"What is it? What's next for you, Tom? What's the answer?"

"God, I wish I knew."[3]

Drugs are able to fill the void and numb this emptiness for a season, but eventually the honeymoon phase wears off and the low-grade gnawing emptiness returns. We start doing more and more, different combinations of drugs, and eventually are doing things we swore we'd never touch. It takes us hostage, and we willingly give up our families, possessions, passions, and everything else we once held dear just to feel normal again. The substance that once gave you pleasure, comfort, and a deep sense of okayness now has a diluted effect or has stopped working altogether. It doesn't

---

[3] *60 Minutes*, season 51, episode 18, Tom Brady interviewed by Steve Kroft, on CBS, June 2005, https://www.cbsnews.com/news/transcript-tom-brady-part-3/

matter how much you put into your lungs, nose, or veins; they just don't do the trick anymore. You're looking for something more. You have joined Ben Harper in realizing "the drugs don't work" and the Rolling Stones' observation "I can't get no satisfaction."

This emptiness is the human experience. Whether you are a drug addict, a quarterback, a business owner, or a stay-at-home mom, you feel it. What is the real answer?

A Knock at the Door

In active heroin addiction, there often came times when I'd run out of my supply. After I'd desperately tapped all other options, I would often turn to the residue from stale pieces of cotton I'd filtered past shots through. After gathering dozens of these brown cottons, some that I had taken through this process many times already, I'd put them into a spoon and filter warm tap water through them into the syringe in hopes of getting some sort of buzz. As I pushed the warm water into my bloodstream, the sickness would momentarily subside before I was instantly back to the flu-like symptoms dope sickness always brought. It never satisfied.

This is a picture of drug addiction. We spend our lives collecting weak pleasures in vain attempts of satisfying our soul sickness to no avail. Life has lost its flavor. We have lost our zeal for living and our ability to dream. Hope is lost. Food doesn't taste as good, our old enjoyments have faded, relationships matter little, and we feel as if life is no longer worthy to be lived.

After some time, the phone would always ring again alerting me to the reality of the pleasure I've been longing for once again. "I'll be over in a minute," my dealer would say. My stomach would twist and turn while waiting for a knock at the door that would signal the cotton washing was over and the real stuff was here. You may have been waiting for that knock for decades.

I believe this book is the knock you've *really* been waiting for. The knock of a lifetime by the pleasure you've been literally dying for. Not the type of temporary pleasure that slowly murders your body and estranges you from your family, but a greater joy that gives you real life. The joy that is knocking at your door is one that will restore the lost years of destruction and fill your emptiness with rich contentment. Are you ready to put down the stale cotton shots and pick up the good stuff? Are you ready to put down the fleeting pleasures of addiction and answer the door to everlasting joy you were created for?

CHAPTER 2

My Story

"**M**y name is C— Ch— Chr—" I stammered as my heart raced and the shame crept in.

The constant stuttering and ensuing anxiety made my life unbearable. Every morning started with a new plan of how I was going to make it all day without embarrassing myself. Where would I go to eat where I could write my order down? How can I get out of that class where the teacher makes us read out loud? Should I take a zero for the class presentation? How can I look like I have friends without actually having to speak to them? This went on for years.

My family lived in a fairly big house in the suburbs of Raleigh, North Carolina. We had everything we needed and most of what we wanted. My dad worked long hours, and my mom stayed home with my sister and me. From the outside, everything looked like we had it all together, but internally I was a wreck. I could put on a happy face, but I was desperately empty. There seemed to be something missing—like a void that shouldn't be there or a scratch I couldn't itch.

At a very young age, I concluded that if I'm only going to live seventy years or so, I wanted to get the most out of this short life.

I decided to pursue my own pleasure with all of my time, energy, and resources. I started out with fairly innocent endeavors, such as sports and different types of music. I remember jumping from girl to girl and hoping *she* would be the answer to my problems. I remember trying my hardest to be a part of the cool crowd, spending lots of time and money getting the coolest clothes, hoping to find an identity as a "popular kid." I jumped headfirst into anything that could possibly fill the void, but nothing worked. I eventually got into more destructive practices

The First High

One day, after failing miserably to hide my speech impediment from the world, some guys asked if I wanted to smoke weed with them. I was eager to participate. As we were sitting in the woods in our middle-class neighborhood, they pulled out a Coke can with holes poked in it and a bag of overly dry weed. *Very classy, eh?* We all took turns passing this Coke can around. *Inhale. Cough. Cough. Cough. Cough!* I didn't get high this time, but the next time I did, and I loved it!

I'd found my answer! My shoulders lowered and I felt almost human. The emptiness in my soul subsided for a while and a genuine smile leaked to my face. For the first time in my life, I felt okay in my own skin. Smoking weed soon became an everyday escape. It became my source of happiness and peace. It's what I lived for.

I always confidently declared weed was the only drug I'd ever do, but I soon found it was a slippery slope. My plan was to grow up to be a hippie stoner and maybe even grow some dreadlocks. I would grow tons of good bud and wear Birkenstocks forever. That vision didn't last long. Some opportune relationships gave me access to any drug I desired. I was like a kid in a candy store. I started dabbling in other drugs. Adderall, Xanax, shrooms, acid,

Klonopin, cocaine, hydrocodone, ecstasy, molly, OxyContin, and eventually heroin. It honestly seemed like overnight I went from weed to heroin. That process is kind of a blur to me now. What I do know is that I didn't care how bad the reputation of the drug was. I was down. If it helped me escape from the anxiety and emptiness, I was eager to try it.

I soon learned what I liked and what I didn't. The uppers, such as cocaine, crack, meth, and Adderall, didn't do the trick for me. Can you imagine a kid who stutters on cocaine? I spent the entire high excitedly trying to tell stories but stuttering so badly that I couldn't get a word out. I can laugh about it now, but it was terrible—both for me and the people I was using with. Downers, on the other hand, such as Xanax, Klonopin, OxyContin, and heroin, did the trick for me. It felt like instant paradise but then forever slavery.

I began selling weed to pay for these other habits. I not only had an answer to emptiness, but I also found purpose and identity. I was the guy who had the best weed and could get his hands on anything you wanted. However, these favorable aspects cast a dark shadow.

What started out as a means of treating my emptiness and comforting my soul quickly turned into the very cancer that was destroying my life. The external aspects of my life began to look a lot like my internal state. My parents got a divorce, I rarely went to school, and I began getting into more serious trouble. My heart was in love. Getting high consumed my mind. I was enslaved. I knew I needed to stop or I wasn't going to see my twenties, so I checked myself into a mental hospital. The exit ramp was not nearly as enjoyable as the on-ramp.

The First of Many Attempts to Pump the Brakes

I was sixteen years old and my first attempt at freedom from heroin had landed me in a mental hospital.

"Let me out of here!" I shouted.

As I looked around this white-walled prison, the other patients were a vision into my future if nothing changed. Hollow humans trapped internally and externally against their will. I had never felt anything this terrible! Intense aches aggravated what seemed like every cell in my body. The flu had nothing on this! Desperate cravings, intense rage and constant complaining led the doctors to pump me full of Seroquel and other psychiatric tranquilizers that made me feel like a zombie but did nothing to fill the void or take away the withdrawals. Sleep evaded me, and the blank hallways seemed to get smaller with each waking hour.

After three days of intense suffering, I raced out the doors and the glaring sun irritated my eyes like warm vinegar had been splashed in them. My parents and I had a handful of medical records with pages of official jargon that ultimately said, "He is a drug addict." How insightful. I immediately went back to getting high.

The Death Needle

When snorting the heroin no longer had the same effect as it once had, I started using a needle, which brought new levels of euphoria as well as new levels of destruction. After the first stick, everything in my life turned three shades darker. Heroin was my god, and I served it faithfully. I was in love, but the object of my affection was out to kill me.

Life was a roller coaster of the highest of highs and the lowest of lows. The most epic feelings of intense pleasure were followed by the darkest feelings of desperation, sometimes for no reason at all. The external consequences were also devastating. I couldn't keep a job. Health issues. I sold drugs to support my habit. Many of my friends overdosed and died. Legal issues. Stealing. No real friends. Gang violence. Robbing and being robbed. Even car wrecks.

When Reality Hits

After a couple days of being without any heroin, I finally got the call from my dealer that I could come get some more. He lived across the street from a church, so instead of waiting until I got home, I shot up in the church parking lot. I wouldn't recommend this.

I made it halfway home before falling asleep at the wheel, running a red light on one of the busiest roads in North Raleigh, and causing a multiple-car wreck. Fortunately, no one was seriously injured, but there were kids in some of the cars and many people ended up going to the hospital. Lots of cop cars eventually showed up and I had to do a sobriety test on the side of this busy intersection. I was arrested, interrogated for many hours, and released because I was under eighteen. Up until this point, I had felt somewhat invincible. My consequences had been rather minor, but this punched me in the face and I felt the reality of what my life was becoming. These charges led to my losing my job and stuck with me for nearly a decade.

My life was a mess, but it was about to get even worse.

The Worst Day of My Life

"Beep beep beep beep beep beep beep beep ..."
My dad's alarm clock was tirelessly shouting in the other room. The annoying sound was muffled enough to not wake a sleeping heroin addict for many hours but loud enough to annoy me after my eyes finally unlatched. I rolled over and looked at my clock. It was 10 a.m. Shouldn't he be at work by now? He must have forgotten to cut off the alarm.

I had just moved back in with my dad after a two-month stint in Greenville, North Carolina, that didn't turn out so well. I moved away with hopes of starting a new life, but the darkness followed, just like each time before. I had turned the new place into another toxic environment. I was glad to be home again with Dad.

He was my rock. Whenever I was in any kind of trouble financially, legally, medically, etc., he always came to the rescue. He was like my best friend.

After I was finally annoyed enough to get out of bed, I stumbled through the living room. When I hit the threshold of my dad's room, there was an eerie feeling that everything was about to change.

I walked to the other side of the bed and the most awful feeling of terror rushed through my frail body. "Dad! *Dad! Dad!*" Frantic tears rushed down my face as I shook him and begged him to wake up.

Nothing.

I called 911.

Raw screams.

The most cutting and intense emotions ripped through my body. The panic-stricken pressure came out in tears and screams like a teakettle glued to a bright-red stovetop. He had had a massive heart attack and had been dead for hours.

This was the most alone I'd ever felt. This was not a game. This was final.

What part had I played in this?

After he passed, I was put in charge of his estate and given way too much money for a twenty-year-old junkie to manage. I had everything I'd ever wanted materially but was still empty on the inside. Within eighteen months, I had spent nearly everything and had destroyed the lives of many people around me. My family wouldn't talk to me, and even my drug addict friends wouldn't talk to me anymore. The girl I was living with was working at a strip club, sleeping with our drug dealer, and overdosing regularly. I finally broke.

The End of the Beginning

A week before Christmas, my mom graciously invited me over for dinner, knowing I probably hadn't eaten in days.

"Chris, aren't you done yet?"

Tears ran down my mom's face, and they started to stream down mine as well. She said, "You're twenty years old. Your dad's money is almost gone. When it's gone, there won't be anybody to take care of you. Your stripper girlfriend has almost died twice this week. Is this the life you want?"

I didn't answer immediately, but blurry images of distant hopes flashed through my mind. This isn't what I wanted for my life.

"Do you want to give life one more chance?"

I'd been to treatment many times before. What would be different about this time? Maybe something would get better.

"I guess," I reluctantly muttered.

We walked upstairs and began to search online for affordable drug treatment.

"Look. There's one in New York."

My mom had obviously never experienced heroin withdrawals. "Too cold."

"How about Florence, South Carolina?"

That's pretty close. Fairly warm. "Okay."

It's amazing the admissions director could understand me through the streaming tears, hopeless tone, and raw stammers.

"We'll see you tomorrow," he said after nearly an hour of broken conversation with an overly hopeful tone.

My mom and I hugged longer than we had since I was a little boy.

I walked out the door into the cool December night, went straight to the ATM, cleared my account, and called my dealer. If this was the last time I was going to get high, I would go out with a bang!

A New Place and a New Season

When we arrived at the treatment center the next day, I stood nearly six feet tall and weighed a sickly one hundred pounds. Fresh track marks from dirty needle pokes crowded my skeleton-like tatted arms. The drugs had become ineffective at filling the gaping hole in my soul that I had felt since I was a little boy. I spent the last five years ringing the pleasures of this world dry, but the unceasing emptiness remained. As we pulled up the gravel driveway, my palms began to sweat. "What am I doing? Why did I agree to this again?"

I stumbled out of the car, still feeling the effects of the three bags of heroin, a couple of bong hits, and the last dozen or so Xanax and Klonopin. My tattered jeans, undersized Bob Marley T-shirt, and dark eyes didn't do justice to show the chaos inside. I had nowhere else to go and no more strings left to pull.

After the intake process, which must have taken much longer than most due to the perpetual nodding out, some of the more tenured residents walked me into the newcomer building. A meeting was in progress as we walked in the creaky door. The owner of the facility who was teaching the meeting made eye contact with me and I quickly looked away as we headed to my room. "That is death walking," he declared to the room full of addicts when he thought I was far enough away to not hear him.

He was right. There was no life in me; I was a walking dead man! The whole reason I started using drugs in the first place was to fill the void I felt inside, but somehow drugs had actually intensified this longing. I was hopeless and empty, and I had been for as long as I could remember.

The Knock I Was Waiting For

"Do you want to go to church with me?" one of the residents asked.

Why would I want to go to church? I don't belong in a place like that. But I will get to leave the rehab for a few hours. I've already been here for a week. Maybe there will be cute girls there.

"It's Christmas Eve. Come on!"

"Okay, I'm in," I said reluctantly.

As we walked into the church, I felt a little out of place but quickly made my way to a seat as the service started.

"Do you feel like you're too messy for God?"

"Does nothing you've tried seem to fill the emptiness in your soul?"

"Do you want a fresh start to life?"

The speaker's words seemed to penetrate my heart like nothing I'd ever experienced. I'd heard messages like this before, but this time, it was as if God was real and was speaking directly to me. He talked about Jesus as a real person. He explained how God loves broken people and that He made a way for people like me to be forgiven and changed. I don't really remember much else He said, but I knew I needed it. I *wanted* it.

I responded as a man dying of thirst in the desert was given the opportunity for a cold glass of water. I made the decision to give up my old life completely and place my trust in Jesus Christ. Tears streamed down my face as I prayed with a tall, lanky guy with a bright-red beard. As we prayed, I got a taste of the joy I'd always wanted. It was like a man who hadn't eaten in years was given a juicy filet mignon. It felt like how it would be if I ever got to see my dad again: pure jubilation, but in an even more perfect and divine way. What I had been looking for was not more drugs, sex, or money; it was God. He was what my soul had been longing for my entire life. This was the knock at the door that I had been dying for.

I've never been the same since. This night began the freedom journey I've been on ever since. Now that I had gotten a taste of the joy I was looking for, my mind and body had to catch up.

Over the next few years, I went through a process of learning how to follow Jesus, stumbling, and getting back up. This hasn't been an overnight process and definitely hasn't been easy, but I haven't used since this night because I've got a greater joy. I have found lifelong freedom, and I desperately want you to experience this same transformation.

I'm not talking about some pie in the sky type of spiritual optimism or religious legalism but a real God who is able to change your life permanently. For lots of people like you and me, the idea of God may seem very lofty and weird, but I'm asking you to give it a chance. What do you have to lose? I wasn't raised in the church and didn't really have any real view of God. I wouldn't have believed any of this unless it worked for me, but it has. That's what led me to write this book.

In the remaining chapters, I am going to lay out how you can experience this transformation. Will you take the time to finish the rest of the book? Will you be open-minded and willing to read about a different way?

Will you answer the knock at the door?

> Behold, I stand at the door and knock. If anyone hears my voice and opens the door, I will come in to him and eat with him, and he with me. (Jesus in Revelation 3:20)

CHAPTER 3

The Most Important Chapter You'll Ever Read

What if our problem isn't that we are addicted to pleasure but that the object of our addiction isn't good enough to satisfy our souls? What if the drugs aren't a strong enough pleasure? What if you were made for a greater joy?[4]

C. S. Lewis, the famous author of *The Chronicles of Narnia*, wrote,

> If we consider the unblushing promises and
> staggering nature of rewards found in the Gospels,
> it would seem that Our Lord finds our desires
> not too strong, but too weak. We are half-hearted
> creatures, fooling about with drink and sex and

---

[4] John Piper, "Passion for the Supremacy of God, Part 2" (preached at Passion Conference in Austin, TX on January 3, 1997), https://www.desiringgod.org/messages/is-christian-hedonism-valid.

ambition when infinite joy is offered us, like an ignorant child who wants to go on making mud pies in a slum because he cannot imagine what is meant by the offer of a holiday at the sea. We are far too easily pleased."[5]

The sad state of people like you and me is that many will spend their entire lives jumping from slum to slum while looking for better mud. They have decided that the best life could be is an updated version of what they are currently experiencing—a different mixture of drugs, a different sexual partner, a new city, more money, etc. They know the mud isn't fun anymore, but they don't know what to do. They try to put it down, but they always end up with dirty hands once again.

What if there is something better? What if there is a holiday at sea available?

What if our problem isn't that we are looking for pleasure too much but that we need to find a better object of our addiction?

The Real Answer to Our Emptiness

Have you ever looked at the sky as the sun is setting? The vibrant oranges and deep purples create a new piece of artwork in the sky every evening that far exceeds even the work of Picasso or Van Gogh. Imagine if you found a brand-new, magnificent painting hanging in your living room every day. This would imply there is a painter and that he or she was able to break into your house. The sublime artwork in the sky implies there is an artist and He breaks into our world every single day to show off His handiwork. If the artwork trick had been done since you were a child, eventually you might grow numb to the miracle, just as we have.

---

[5] C.S. Lewis, *The Weight of Glory* (New York, NY: Harper Collins, 1949), 26.

Have you ever tasted a warm cup of coffee on a cold day? As you lift your tasty brew to your lips, the heavenly haze breathes into your nose. As the coffee notes hit your taste buds, your brain synapses begin to fire as fresh feelings of delight flood your brain. Have you ever thought about how intricate this process is? On your tongue are 10,000 taste buds that work together with your nose to pick up the delightful notes in the coffee. The complexities of how the brain processes taste are divine!

How about your eyes? Have you ever thought about the intricacies of how your eyes are able to pick up different colors and light, processing them immediately? The magnitude of the Rocky Mountains, the perfectly painted stripes on a tiger, the tiny bones in the human ear, love, family, the might of the ocean, the tartness and tiny hairs of a raspberry, and the breathtaking views of the Grand Canyon all scream, "There is a Creator!" There is something, or mainly someone, behind all of this beauty. This is not just the result of a massive explosion but a creatively designed universe. Order did not and cannot come from chaos. A design implies a designer. There is a God.

This real God has made everything in the universe, including us, to show His beauty and value and for our enjoyment. With all this beauty in the world, He chose humans to be the pinnacle of His creation. We were made in His image to be in a relationship with Him, and in the context of this relationship is where we find peace, security, acceptance, love, belonging, comfort, pleasure, identity, meaning, and yes, joy. Psalm 16:11 says, "In God's presence there is fullness of joy and at His right hand are pleasures forevermore." You were made to live in free joy, like a child playing outside with their daddy, laughing too hard to comprehend why you started in the first place. God's design is for you to be in such unity with Him that you have no addiction, no fear, perfect identity, clear purpose, and feel completely okay in your own skin.

We see this in the opening chapters of the Bible. In Genesis 1–2, we get a picture of how life was meant to be. The first two humans, Adam and Eve, had a perfect relationship with God and with each other. They were "naked and unashamed," which means they didn't have anything to hide. Can you imagine that? There was no anxiety or emptiness, and they felt okay in their own skin. Their first full day was a day of rest, which means we were created to have rest for our souls. "God blessed them" and then gave them a purpose to "be fruitful and multiply and fill the earth and subdue it." You and I were made for this ideal experience of being human— to live in intimacy with God and each other; to have no shame and be okay with being truly known; to be blessed by God and have a rested soul; and to have meaningful purpose that wakes us up in the morning with passion. You were made for this holiday at sea.

Mud Pies in the Slum

As we can tell, something has gone terribly wrong with this perfect plan. Every time we cut on the news, there is another report of a school shooting, race-motivated murders, overdoses, and political conflict. Rather than living in perfect relationship with God and others, people are separated from God and conflicted with each other. Rather than living in the fullness of joy in a holiday at sea, we are playing with unsatisfying mud pies in a slum. The Bible tells us this happened because of sin, which is simply anything that's against God. Our rebellion against Him started with the first humans in the garden of Eden when Adam and Eve went against the commands of God, choosing the creation over the Creator (Romans 1). God told them they could eat from any tree in the garden of Eden except one: the Tree of the Knowledge of Good and Evil. The serpent tricked the humans into going against the commands of God, thinking they could become like Him. They thought they were smarter than God and thought they'd be better at ruling their lives. The consequences were devastating. The "naked and unashamed" life immediately led to a deep sense of shame and them hiding who they really were from each other. They reacted to this shame just like we do: by trying to cover it up (religion) and run away from God (rebellion). The intimacy with God was broken, and they felt emptiness for the first time. The blessing and peace were replaced with anxiety and constant struggle. They chose the mud pies of the forbidden fruit over the holiday at sea of intimacy with God. From this point on, humanity has faced massive consequences.

Because of Adam and Eve's sin, you and I are born in sin. It's not something we learn but who we are from birth. My sister and I violently screaming over the front seat is a perfect example of this depravity. No one taught us how to be this selfish; we were born that way. Sin isn't just something we do, but it's who we are at our core. Because of this, every person is born separated from God. This separation leaves us empty, searching for pleasure anywhere we can find a taste (alcohol, sex, popularity, power, drugs, etc.). This is why we feel the void deep in our souls. As we continue to indulge in these faux pleasures, our hearts, minds, and bodies become more and more enslaved. This is what drug addiction is: *running to anything other than God in order to fill our vacancies, which eventually enslaves our hearts, minds, and bodies.* Like a straitjacket, the more we fight, the tighter it gets. We are like that ignorant child jumping from slum to slum while playing with different types of mud and hoping to eventually find the one that actually works. You may have been searching for years.

The Bible is very clear that sin leads to death (Romans 6:23). Drug addicts understand this better than almost anyone. We've tasted death through personal overdose, car wrecks, or the loss of someone close to us. Sin will always eventually lead to physical death, but it also is the means of spiritual and eternal death. The New Testament describes it like this:

And you were dead in the trespasses and sins
in which you once walked, following the course

of this world, following the prince of the power of the air, the spirit that is now at work in the sons of disobedience—among whom we all once lived in the passions of our flesh, carrying out the desires of the body and the mind, and were by nature children of wrath, like the rest of mankind. (Ephesians 2:1–3)

Because God is perfectly holy and completely just, His wrath is on all sin—including us. All of the power that holds the universe together is aimed against sin. If we die in this state, we will be eternally separated from God in hell. First Corinthians 6:10 clearly says that unforgiven and unchanged alcoholics and drug addicts will not enter the kingdom of God.

Many have realized their need for God and have begun climbing the ladder of religion while hoping to earn their way back to Him. Many programs and religions focus on this approach. Their mantras are "What can I do to unblock myself from God? What must I do to earn right standing with God?" In my opinion, this is a worse condition than the first. At least sin is fun for a season. Dead religion is not (except for the pious pride that dimly sparks some sort of mediocre pleasure.) Earning God's approval back on our power is impossible. It's like trying to jump from my house in South Carolina to Antarctica. Even if I trained my whole life to become an Olympic long jumper, I will not be much closer. There is no way to escape the consequences of our sin or to get right with God by our own effort, steps, or religiosity. Like a man who accidentally falls in quicksand, the more we fight, the deeper we seem to sink.

A Loving Father

The good news about God is He is not just a Holy Judge but also a Loving Father who cares deeply about you. Rather than leaving us in our desperate condition, He made a way that we can be saved from our sin and brought back into a right relationship with Him to live the abundant life He has promised. He made a way that we can return to the beauty we see in His original design. He sent His Son, Jesus Christ, to pay for all the wrong we've done and who we are apart from Christ. Jesus is a real, historical person, unlike the fairy-tale stories we heard as kids of the Easter bunny and Santa Claus. He was born to a virgin woman, came to earth fully God and fully man, and lived a perfect life in our place. He spent most of his time with the outcasts of society (sick, prostitutes, and even addicts) like us, claiming that He is God, healing them, and telling them their sin can be forgiven.

Jesus said crazy things like "Those who are well have no need of a physician, but those who are sick. I came not to call the righteous, but sinners" (Mark 2:17), which made the religious people of his day very angry. Claiming to be the Savior and long-awaited Messiah, He said, "God has sent me to proclaim liberty to the captives and recovering of sight to the blind, to set at liberty those who are oppressed" (Luke 4:18). The religious elite eventually had enough and Jesus was arrested, beaten, whipped, spit on, and murdered. Large spikes were hammered through his hands and feet to nail him to a piece of wood in the shape of a cross—one of the most brutal torture devices in history. This is the punishment that you and I deserve, but He took the punishment on Himself instead. "For while we were still sinners Christ died for us" (Romans 5:8).

After Jesus was proven dead, He was put in a tomb, but He did not stay there long. On the third day, in the most important moment in human history, Jesus literally rose from the grave. By doing this, Jesus proved all He said was true, including His claims to be God. Sin (including addiction) and death were defeated. This is the gospel. God loves you so much that He sent His Son, Jesus, to live a perfect life in your place, die the death you deserve, and be raised from the dead to raise you into brand-new life of freedom.

> For God so loved the world so much that he gave
> his only Son, that whoever believes in him should
> not perish, but have eternal life. (John 3:16)

This is the answer to addiction. Addiction is slavery to anything other than God, but now we are free to be addicted to God.

Our Response

The only right response to this is to repent and believe. This means to turn away from your old way of life and trust Jesus Christ's life, death, and resurrection for your right standing with God. It's a complete change of mind and heart when it comes to God. When this truly occurs, you will be reconciled to God. Like the child who puts down the mud to enjoy the holiday at sea, you will begin to taste the joys of a restored relationship with God. Your sin is cast out as far as the east is from the west (Psalm 103:12). The Judge's gavel has declared you innocent at the expense of His own Son. This means you no longer need to earn God's approval, but you can live in freedom knowing you are fully loved, completely forgiven, and eternally secure. God is no longer our enemy but our Friend and our Master. This does not mean life will be easy, but it does mean that you will have God and He will be enough regardless of your circumstances. You will begin to experience life as God originally designed it.

Jesus offers a picture of what this looks like in Matthew 13:45–46. "The kingdom of heaven is like a merchant in search of fine pearls, who, on finding one pearl of great value, went and sold all that he had and bought it." You have been in search of fine pearls your whole life. When you finally see God for the treasure He is, you will turn away from everything else, including drugs, to be with Him forever. Jesus told a similar parable. "The

Kingdom of Heaven is like treasure hidden in a field, in which a man found and covered up. Then in his joy he goes and sells all he has and buys that field" (Matthew 13:44). I love how Jesus says "in his joy …" This means repenting and believing isn't done out of begrudging submission but is an act of joy because we have seen how incredible life with God could be. It's not divorcing the spouse you love for one of lesser value but forsaking all others because you get to marry the person of your dreams!

Another man who had a very sketchy past, Paul, echoes this in Philippians 3:7–8. "But whatever gain I had, I counted as loss for the sake of Christ. Indeed, I count everything as loss because of the surpassing worth of knowing Christ Jesus my Lord. For his sake I have suffered the loss of all things and count them as rubbish, in order that I may gain Christ." Because of the "surpassing worth of knowing Christ," Paul gave up all of his past religious accomplishments and things he held dear in order to have a relationship with Christ. Intimacy with God is worth whatever you must give up to repent and believe in Jesus!

True salvation is not just praying an empty prayer or trying to be more religious by going to church or trying to not use drugs. It is placing all of your hopes of life on earth and the afterlife on what Jesus did on the cross. It means surrendering your whole life to Jesus, trusting He is worth it. Jesus is inviting you into this restored relationship with Him right now.

> Repent therefore, and turn back, that your sins may be blotted out, that times of refreshing may come from the presence of the Lord … (Acts 3:19–20)

> Come, everyone who thirsts, come to the waters; and he who has no money, come, buy and eat! Come, buy wine and milk without money and without price. (Isaiah 55:1)

This is the offer of a holiday at sea.

This is the knock at the door you've been waiting for.

After many years of experiencing life with God, I am pleading with you to not settle for mud pies anymore! Don't waste another day settling for mediocre pleasures when infinite joy is offered! Repent from unsatisfying sin and dead religion and be saved! This is the answer you've been looking for. This is the pleasure you've literally been dying for.

If you are ready to repent of your sin and place your faith in Jesus Christ, you can pray something like the prayer that's written below. God is listening, and He is eager to save you. Get alone, and pray this from the most genuine place in your heart. It's not the prayer that saves you; it's the faith behind the prayer that saves you.

Dear Heavenly Father,

I know I have sinned against You and have not wanted anything to do with You.

I am sorry I have worshipped drugs and other mediocre gods rather than You.

I know I can't save myself, and I can't earn back Your approval.

But I believe that You can save me. I want You to save me.

I believe You died on the cross in my place. I believe You rose from the dead.

I repent of my sin, and I place my faith in You.

I give You everything.

Take over my life. Fill me with Your Spirit. Lead me for the rest of my life.

Please save me now. I love You, Jesus.

Action

1. Genuinely repent and pray the above prayer while giving your whole life to Jesus.
2. Find someone who you know is living for Jesus and tell them what just happened.
3. Ask that person or a church nearby to baptize you.

CHAPTER 4

The New You

My eyes opened to a Christmas unlike any other. I was still in rehab and my body ached from the withdrawals. There were no presents under the tree, but I had just received the best gift of my life.

Christmas was always a festive day in my house as a kid. The tallest tree in the county was covered in ornaments collected through the decades. Our stockings were pregnant with gifts. Dad and I set up the tiny clay snow village. Mistletoe hung above the doorway, and the scent of Mom's holiday ham permeated the house. Piles of wrapped presents showed that St. Nick had come by. (I must have fooled him again.) Family traditions filled the day as distant relatives stopped by. It was the day I looked forward to each year with grand expectations.

This year was different. The stiff, cardboard-like sheets were soaked in sweat. My family was replaced with dozens of addicts, and the few decorations from the dollar store paled in comparison to the ones I knew as a kid. The smell was less like Christmas bliss and more like body odor. The food was a small step up from what we normally ate. I was a little over a hundred pounds, my heart was still pounding, and my mind was still racing. But something was different. I had something I hadn't had in a very long time, if ever. I didn't need the decorations because I had the joy of Christmas inside me. The gifts I received as a child would satisfy for a moment, but this gift is one that keeps on giving.

If you've given your life to Christ, you know how I felt that Christmas morning. Your circumstances haven't changed, your body may still need to be detoxed, your mind is still spinning, but something is vastly different.

The Prodigal Son

In one of the most famous parables in the Bible, Jesus tells a story showing what happens when we begin a relationship with God and what gifts He gives us. A son of a wealthy man asks for his inheritance and leaves home to go find happiness. He wastes it on partying, prostitutes, and possibly drugs. He eventually runs out of money, there is a famine, and he gets a job feeding pigs. In the Jewish context, feeding pigs was about the worst job he could get. He hits rock bottom and begins to dream of home. His dad. The food. Even his older brother. The emptiness of the pigpen and the longing for home become too great, and he begins his long journey home.

As he trudges the shameful journey home, he plans his amends. *I'll be your servant until I pay back everything I spent. I will sleep outside and work overtime until it's paid back.* As he approaches the house, his dad comes running. His dad never ran. The young man braced himself for the scolding. "But while he was still a long way off, his father saw him and felt compassion, and ran and embraced him and kissed him" (Luke 15:21). Rather than a beating, he was met with a joyful embrace.

This is God's response to you and every other person, drug addict or not, who comes home. Even though you've spent most of your life wanting nothing to do with Him and wasting your days in reckless living, He receives you back home with overwhelming joy.

The father not only receives him back but also showers him with gifts as if it was Christmas morning. Each one illustrates an aspect of the son's new identity. Like a father who's adopting a child, who gives them a birth certificate, social security card, and a new last name, these gifts are crucial to your future. God is showing us what changed when we ran into His arms. Just like a kid of Christmas morning, open each of these gifts with joy and expectation.

Robe

"But the father said to his servants, 'Bring quickly the best robe, and put it on him ...'" (Luke 15:22)

The son shows up in dirty rags wreaking of pig dung and last night's party, but his dad clothes him in an expensive robe made for a prince. This is a picture of how Jesus covers our shame and clothes us in His perfect righteousness. When we come to God, we are polluted with shame and the stench of our life of sin. Just like Adam and Eve in the garden, our natural reaction is to hide our shame, but God killed an animal to cover their nakedness, and He does the same for us. Jesus was killed so that you can be clothed in His righteousness.

"[God] chose us in him before the foundation of the world, that we should be holy and blameless before him" (Ephesians 1:4). In active drug addiction, you most likely have done some things that you aren't proud of—sexual deviances, hurting family members, abortion, secret sins, etc. No matter how dirty you were when you came to Jesus, you are now completely clean and totally covered. Read that last sentence again. With one touch from Jesus, you've been made clean. Everything you've ever done is paid for. "Come now, let us reason together, says the LORD: though your sins are like scarlet, they shall be as white as snow; though they are red like crimson, they shall become like wool" (Isaiah 1:18).

Before I asked my wife to marry me, we went on a walk and I told her every wretched thing I'd ever done. I told her some very embarrassing and depraved things. I will never forget her response after I timidly shared the laundry list of things I had hoped to take to my grave. "That's not who you are anymore. That's not how Jesus sees you, and that's not how I see you. I see you as holy and blameless."

All of your past was put on Jesus on the cross, and all of His righteousness is given to you. You are no longer what you did. You no longer have to walk around in shame because of what you did last week, last year, or when you were a kid. You have been washed, sanctified, and justified (1 Corinthians 6:11). You are perfectly righteous. As you accept this clean slate, you can hold your head high while knowing that you have nothing to hide.

Ring

"And put a ring on his hand ..." (Luke 15:22)

This symbolizes full acceptance and authority as a son.[6] The young son was hoping to be accepted as one of the hired servants, but his father gives him the family signet ring, fully restoring him into the family. Likewise, you are now a child of God.

> But to all who did receive him, who believed in his name, he gave the right to become children of God, who were born, not of blood nor of the will of the flesh nor of the will of man, but of God. (John 1:12–13)

---

[6] Matthew Henry, *Commentary on the Whole Bible: Genesis to Revelation*, Edited by Leslie F Church, New one vol. ed. (Grand Rapids: Zondervan Pub. House, 1978).

You don't have to try to pay for what you've done through good works, and you don't have to earn a relationship with God through taking religious steps. But you are fully a child of God, and you have a perfect relationship with Him right now.

You may have some skewed views of what the word *dad* means, depending on your upbringing. Your dad may have been abusive, passive, or distant, or you may not even know him. Whatever your earthly dad was like, your Heavenly Father is better. He never flies off the handle, and He won't ever leave you or abandon you. You can trust him fully. He's adopted you, and you are now a part of His family forever.

Like many adoption stories, there is sometimes a behavioral learning curve. The old way of doing things in your former life will sometimes bleed into the new. I had, and still have, quite a few old habits and mind-sets that do not line up with how things work in God's family. God is always patient and will lovingly discipline you like any loving dad.

Knowing this aspect of your identity is the difference between the fear of going into court to face a judge for charges you know you are guilty of and the playful exuberance of a young child jumping into their father's arms. You can climb into your dad's lap today and every day to experience the joy of intimacy with Him, rather than walking on eggshells trying to appease the judge. Anytime you are empty, you can run to God to experience the joy of relationship with your dad.

This ring also symbolized that even though he wasted his first inheritance, his father was planning on giving him another one. You also have an inheritance because you are a coheir with Christ. Your inheritance is the entire universe, which means that you no longer have to selfishly manipulate people, places, and things to get more for yourself. You can freely give, knowing that in Christ, you already own everything!

Your new birth certificate says "child of God," and you have access to all the benefits.

THE REAL ANSWER TO ADDICTION

Shoes

"And shoes on his feet." (Luke 15:22)

The son likely had sold everything he owned, including his shoes. As he walked home barefoot, his feet were likely bloody and disgusting. The father giving him shoes was for his future purpose and the difficult seasons ahead. He was equipping him for everything he'd do and experience. God's plan for your life far exceeds your current plans. If He told you everything you'd do for Him and the opposition you'd face, it'd probably be too much for you to handle at one time. You don't need to know exactly what your future holds, but you do need to know that He has equipped you for every single thing we will face in the future (Hebrews 13:21). He has put shoes on your feet and equipped you for the battles to come.

The other meaning of these shoes is that in Jesus's day, the feet were the most disgusting part of the person's body. Imagine how disgusting this son's feet would have been after trudging through pig dung for many months, hardly ever taking a shower, and walking many miles back to his father's house. And my wife thinks my feet stink? I think the fact that the father gave his son shoes was a picture of how God covers the worst part of us. Most of us have those one or two (or twenty) things that we plan on taking to our grave. Maybe a weird sexual experience, something we did when we were drunk, or something we did for drugs when we were very desperate. Jesus died to cover that! I think this is one of the same reasons Jesus washed the disciples' feet right before being arrested and murdered. He wants you and me to know that there is nothing too gross for Him.

Feast

"And bring the fattened calf and kill it, and let us eat and celebrate." (Luke 15:23)

When the son left home, he was looking to get his fill in the world, but he ended up starving in a pigpen. The feast he was looking for was back at his dad's house the whole time. When he finally came home, they called together all their friends, played loud music, and feasted on the richest foods the father had been saving for a special occasion. It was likely the whole village was at this party. The closest example we have of this is likely what happens when a baseball team wins the World Series. Jumping, cheering, dancing, and even corks poppin'! Pure elation.

I always thought drugs would be the peak of my partying days, but God has shown me that the joy I've experienced since becoming an apprentice of Jesus is way more satisfying than anything I ever experienced in addiction. The pleasure I was seeking in drugs is now on my plate every day in Christ. Jesus gives us a feast with the rarest delicacies and most satisfying delights. He said, "I am the bread of life. Whoever comes to me will never go hungry, and whoever believes in me will never be thirsty" (John 6:25). This feast never runs out. He will satisfy your soul for the rest of eternity.

You are not only treated as a child of God but as the guest of honor. This feast is not a one-time affair; you have access to God Himself forever. He has prepared a table before you. The prophet Isaiah echoes this.

> Come, everyone who thirsts,
> come to the waters;
> and he who has no money,
> come, buy and eat!
> Come, buy wine and milk
> without money and without price.
> Why do you spend your money for that which is not bread,
> and your labor for that which does not satisfy?
> Listen diligently to me, and eat what is good,
> and delight yourselves in rich food. (Isaiah 55:1–2)
> Eat your fill!

Life

"For this my son was dead, and is alive again ..." (Luke 15:24)

The father continues to explain what has happened to his son with this declaration. Not only was the son lost and is now found, but he was dead and is now alive. You too used to be dead *in* your sins, but now you are dead *to* sin.

> We know that our old self was crucified with him in order that the body of sin might be brought to nothing, so that we would no longer be enslaved to sin. For one who has died has been set free from sin. (Romans 6:6–7)

When Jesus rose from the grave, the power of sin and death was completely broken for everyone who is in Christ. The chains have been cut, and the prison doors are wide open. You are no longer a slave to drugs. "So you also must consider yourselves dead to sin and alive to God in Christ Jesus" (Romans 6:11).

When you received Christ, you became a new creation (2 Corinthians 5:17). God has changed your very nature, like a caterpillar to a butterfly. The old you is no longer alive, but the new you is here to stay. You've been reborn. He's started changing you from the inside out. Before Christ, you were in love with yourself and the world, but now you'll notice yourself loving God and others. It's a beautifully strange experience when you begin wanting to read the Bible, pray, serve others, and even give away your money and possessions to those less fortunate than you. John Piper says this is like getting new spiritual taste buds for the things of God.[7] This new life isn't mediocre but abundant. Jesus said, "The thief comes only to steal and kill and destroy. I came

---

[7] John Piper, "The Danger: Perishing," December 4, 1994, on *Desiring God*, https://www.desiringgod.org/messages/the-danger-perishing.

that they may have life and have it abundantly" (John 10:10). You are dead to sin and abundantly alive to God in Christ!

God has welcomed you home, giving you a new identity and a new nature. For some of us, this may seem too good to be true because in every other area of our lives, our actions determine our reward. What we do determines what we get. Let's go back to the adoption illustration one more time. When a child is adopted, instantly their last name changes. Without doing anything right or changing any of their behavior or value system, they get a new identity. It is very likely their value system doesn't line up with the value system of the family adopting them, but that doesn't dictate whether they are legally a part of that family. For the next five, ten, fifteen, twentysomething years, the child will be conformed into the image of his new family. This is how your new identity works as well. You have been adopted into the new family and you have a new identity! This happens immediately and isn't determined by your actions or values. Now you will begin the lifelong process of adopting kingdom family values and behaviors!

When the pigpen is calling you back and the memories of mud pies try to pull you back into your old life, you can know that's not who you are anymore. You are righteous. You are a child of God. You are equipped for everything coming your way. You have a table before you to feast on the rarest delicacies. You are dead to sin. You are a new creation. Unwrap these gifts and treat every day as Christmas morning, knowing you've been given these sublime presents.

Your nature has been changed, but if you're going to experience lasting freedom, this new nature must infect every area of your life. Addiction not only affects your spiritual nature but also your heart, mind, and body. Before we were in Christ, we had no choice in our addiction because we had a sin nature. We were enslaved. Our heart was in love with drugs, our mind was set on the flesh, and our body served sin. Now the core of who you are has changed, but your heart, mind, and body must continue to be transformed. How can your heart continue to change into one that fully loves God? How can your mind be renewed to be fully set on the Spirit? How can your body break free from your old habits and serve God wholeheartedly?

For the remainder of this book, you're going to learn how to practically live this out on a daily basis in order to experience ever-increasing joy in God.

Action

1. Find a quiet place to get alone with God for an hour without any technology.
2. During this time, write down who you used to be before you received Jesus. After you have finished this, draw a cross over your list and burn it. The old you has died.
3. Now go back through this chapter and write down your new identity. Who are you now that you are in Christ? Keep this somewhere you can see it every day. The new you is here to stay.

CHAPTER 5

No More Isolation

Johann Hari traveled the world in hopes of finding better ways to help drug addicts. After meeting with dozens of people—experts and junkies alike—he concluded, "The opposite of addiction is not sobriety. The opposite of addiction is connectivity".[8] One of the men he met along his journey is Canadian psychologist Bruce K. Alexander, who conducted a study called Rat Park in the 1970s. He put rats in empty, isolated cages with two water bottles: one with plain water and the other with morphine water. Nearly 100 percent of the time, the rats would become addicted to the drug water and eventually die from an overdose. He also created a giant cage that he called Rat Park that had dozens of rats, cheese, and toys, along with the same two water bottles. It was like the garden of Eden for rats. His studies showed that almost none of the rats in the connected environment became addicted or died. They barely touched the morphine water! After getting some of the rats addicted in the

---

[8] Johann Hari, "Everything You Think You Know About Addiction is Wrong," (lecture, TedGlobalLondon, June 2015), https://www.ted.com/talks/johann_hari_everything_you_think_you_know_about_addiction_is_wrong.

first environment, he moved them to Rat Park. These rats stopped using the drug water very quickly.

Obviously, you are much more than a Canadian rat in a cage, but the principle of connectivity is crucial to our lives. When we are isolated, we are much more likely to use drugs and become addicted, but when we are truly connected, the drugs don't seem as necessary and sustained freedom is possible. I know this from personal experience. Being immersed in raw community has grown my relationship with Jesus and is one of the main reasons I'm still living in freedom today. People have celebrated with me in the best times and been there in the dark hours of the night when throwing my life away and returning to the mud pies seemed like a decent option. Being connected in community has a massive impact on our ability to live and thrive in freedom.

Community is God's plan for our lives. In Acts 2, we get a glimpse of this. During the first ever church service that occurred soon after Jesus ascended into heaven, 3,000 people from all walks of life (some may have had an addiction of one kind or another) responded to the gospel and started following Jesus. This passage gives us an inside look to how these first believers lived their lives connected to one another.

> There were added that day about three thousand souls. And they devoted themselves to the apostles' teaching and **the fellowship**, to the breaking of bread and the prayers. And awe came upon every soul, and many wonders and signs were being done through the apostles. And **all who believed were together** and had all things in common. And they were selling their possessions and belongings and distributing the proceeds to all, as any had need. And day by day, **attending the temple together** and **breaking bread in their homes**, they received their food with glad and

generous hearts, praising God and having favor
with all the people. And the Lord added to their
number day by day those who were being saved
(Acts 2:41–47; emphasis mine).

These new believers knew they couldn't do life alone. They knew they needed each other. After meeting Jesus, they immersed themselves in relationships with other Christians. They ate together, worshipped together, and cared for each other. They hung out almost every day, talked about God, and told others about God together. This is a great example of what it looks like to live in Rat Park.

People who've struggled with addiction need this more than anyone. This is where we can be encouraged, taught, and corrected. It's where we can laugh until it hurts and run when we get trapped in our own heads. It's a place where we can experience more of God. Jesus said, "For where two or three are gathered in my name, there am I among them" (Matthew 18:20).

Community is in our core makeup. In Genesis 1, in the creation account, God said, "Let *us* make man in *our* image." The author intentionally makes this sentence plural to show that we are made for community. What he means by "us" and "our" is the trinity: Father, Son, and Holy Spirit. Three distinct persons are eternally dwelling in perfect unity as one God. We are made in the image of God, and He models perfect community for us with the Father, the Son, and the Holy Spirit. To experience the fullness of life as a human and to be a picture of God, we must live in community. It's what we are made for!

God's original design was for us to have a perfect relationship with Him and a perfect relationship with others. The gospel not only reconciles us back to God, but it also forms us into a family. As we do life with other Christians, our hearts, minds, and bodies will continue to be transformed into who God created us to be.

You may be thinking, *That's great, but all my friends are junkies. Where can I find godly community?* There are many ways you can do this, but I'm going to go into greater detail with three.

1- Church

For thousands of years, Christians have gathered to worship God. The word *church* comes from the Greek word *ekklesia,* which means an assembly or gathering of people. The author of Hebrews encourages,

> And let us consider how to stir up one another to love and good works, not neglecting to meet together, as is the habit of some, but encouraging one another, and all the more as you see the Day drawing near. (Hebrews 10:24–25)

You may have negative experiences in your past with church. Maybe your grandma dragged you to church or your family was hurt by one. Maybe you've never even been to church before. Despite your church history, finding a good church family to be a part of is one of the most crucial aspects of continuing to follow Jesus and living the full life Jesus bought for us.

The church is meant to be a picture of God's kingdom to the rest of the world. It's meant to be a place where Christians gather to worship God and encourage each other. It's a place for healing and growth, correction, and community. The church is the primary vehicle of God's kingdom advancing in the earth. There are some things that only happen when we gather for church, and it's too good of a gift for you to miss out on!

After becoming a Christian, I dove into a church community, and this is still one of the bright spots of my life. Find a church in your area that you can plug into. No church will be perfect, but my advice is to find one that preaches the gospel, teaches the Bible, and makes disciples. You'll likely get hurt, but stick it out for the long haul. Make it a priority to be there as often as possible, and immerse yourself into the community. Don't just attend once a week, but join a small group, start serving, and hang out with other church members as much as possible. Make the early church in Acts 2 your example to follow. How can you utilize a church to make your life look more like Rat Park than an empty isolated cage?

2- 3:00 A.M. Friends

Church is vital, but our connectivity must go deeper. This started for me shortly after arriving at treatment when I met one of my best friends in the world.

> "Hey, Bo! Good morning! It's a great day to be sober!" This man's thick Texas accent boomed into my ears at 6 a.m. across the courtyard. Smiling from ear to ear, he seemed genuinely happy to be alive.

> *Doesn't he know he's at a drug and alcohol treatment facility? Who is this loud human being?*

> "Hey, man. What's up?" I said reluctantly, trying to hide the fact that I wanted to punch him in the face.

> I didn't know this at the time, but this loud, joyful, slightly obnoxious human being would soon become a tool God used to change my life in more ways than I could've imagined.

"Six months ago, some strangers from a twelve-step group put me on a bus to come to South Cackalacki! I love this place!"

He had to be high. How could a homeless crackhead be this happy?

"I've been sober for six months ... That's the longest sober time I've had since I was twelve ... Well, except when I was locked up!" He let out a big belly laugh. "I've got a roof over my head! I've got food in my belly! I got God in my heart! I got all I could ever need!"

I soon realized this was not a show at all. This toothless man had met Jesus a few months before I arrived and was now walking in true freedom—true joy.

Over the next few years, we became best friends.

This type of person is what many people have referred to as a 3 a.m. friend. He's a person I can call at all hours of the night. People who are 3 a.m. friends can be extremely raw with and confess things you hope no one finds out about. People like you and me sometimes have pretty crazy thoughts, especially early on in our freedom journey. Thoughts of using, taboo sexual desires, and much more. If you stuff those thoughts, keeping them to yourself, they may become a reality. Exposing those thoughts strips them of most of their power. Look for someone you can spill your guts to. These aren't social media "friends" who only see the best version of you but people who know the worst parts and love you anyway.

Who we hang out with is who we eventually become. We must take a strong look at the people we are spending the most time with and make some serious changes. "The righteous choose their friends wisely" (Proverbs 12:26). I'd recommend cutting out every addiction relationship for at least a year—even some family members if necessary. I deleted every drug contact I had in my phone. This may seem drastic and may be a very painful process, but I've seen way too many people hold on to unhealthy friendships that led them back to the mud pies and some even to their grave. Jesus said, "Everyone who has left houses or brothers or sisters or father or mother or children or lands, for my name's sake, will receive a hundredfold and will inherit eternal life" (Matthew 19:29). Jesus promises to bless you exponentially for anything you give up to follow Him fully.

Begin spending time with people who are where you want to be. You may find these people at church, in recovery meetings, or other places like a gym. This may take time, but it will be worth it!

3- Spiritual Mentor

In the thirteenth century, Emperor Frederick II of Rome did an experiment that isolated babies from their parents in hopes of determining the original language of man. (Yeah, that dude must've had some serious issues.) The babies were fed and bathed by nurses but were not spoken to or held. Without the love and communication of older humans, the babies all passed away. This is a very sad and evil experiment, but it shows our need for human interaction, especially from people who can take care of us.[9]

This principle is also true in our Christian journey.

Not only do we need godly friends, but also godly mentors. We need more mature Christians, who are typically older and the

---

[9] Willow Winsham, "Emperor Frankenstein: The Truth Behind Frederick II of Sicily's Sadistic Science Experiments," History Answers, August 19, 2017, https://www.historyanswers.co.uk/kings-queens/emperor-frankenstein-the-truth-behind-frederick-ii-of-sicilys-sadistic-science-experiments/.

same gender, to show us how to continue to follow Jesus. They live as examples to us, helping us work through our past and teaching us how to become fully devoted followers of Jesus. Paul emphasizes the need for people like this. "For though you have countless guides in Christ, you do not have many fathers. For I became your father in Christ Jesus through the gospel" (1 Corinthians 4:15). It's a great thing to have pastors and teachers that you learn from afar, but we also need people who know us personally and can help us grow and hold us accountable. Having a world-class chef who cooks the best food in the universe is wonderful, but there must also be someone to teach the child how to eat. In AA and NA programs, these are called sponsors. Christians often call these people "spiritual fathers" or "disciplers."

Early in my relationship with Jesus, it helped to have someone to empathize with my story, but now many of my mentors don't have a past like mine. More mature Christians have much insight to offer us, even if they've never touched a drug. My first mentor and I talked almost daily for the first year, but now I meet with my mentors less often and go to them primarily with more serious situations. They are still a vital part of my life.

Find someone who is much older than you and walking closely with Jesus that you want to pattern your life after. Tell them about the metamorphosis God is doing in your life right now and that you've been advised to find a mentor. They'll likely be glad to help you out. You may ask them to read this book with you and help navigate the work ahead. Finding a good spiritual mentor is one of the most crucial things you can do in this freedom journey. They will be a tool God uses to guide you into more freedom and richer joy.

Community Is Good but Not God

Although community is an indispensable part of our lives, people are not our God. Many addicts become overly dependent on another person—partner, friend, or mentor—only to be disappointed. They can be there for us, but they cannot fill our void. They can encourage us, but they cannot fix our problems. Whenever we try to find in others what only God can give us, we will become discontent and the other person will crumble under the pressure of our praise. Neediness sucks the other person dry of everything they have to give, and we still don't get what we're looking for. People are meant to point us to God, not take His place.

Community works best when we are satisfied in God, looking to Him for our deep sense of okayness. This overflows into healthy relationships with others without being overly needy and dependent on someone other than God. Many sociologists have called this interdependence. At the beginning of our freedom journey, we will need people more than usual for a season, but this should always transition into dependence on God. He is able to stand the test of all of your neediness. He can bear the weight of your worship. Community is a good thing, but it is not our God.

It's Worth It

For years, we have lived like the isolated rats chugging the drug water as fast as we can get it into our bodies. Now God has saved us and adopted us into His family. We can leave the empty cage and join the celebration at Rat Park. As we begin to do life with other people, we will quickly find that community is messy. People will let us down, and vice versa. It won't be easy, but it will be worth it. You'll surely find your heart, mind, and body becoming more like Jesus. Community will help you continue to live in freedom and not return to the mud pies in the slum, as you begin to enjoy this holiday at sea.

Having good community will be especially crucial as we dive into the next chapter and begin to work through the pain of the past.

Action

1. What church are you going to plug into? How can you immerse yourself in this community?
2. How can you find some 3 a.m. friends? Reach out to them and let them know what you are hoping for out of that friendship.
3. Who do you know you need to cut out of your life for a season? Take the necessary action steps to make this a reality.
4. Who is the person you'd like to mentor you? Reach out to them today.

CHAPTER 6

Murdering Your Past

On April 26, 2003, a rock climber named Aron Ralston drove five hours to explore Bluejohn Canyon, Utah, where he spent the day climbing. Just before starting the long journey back to his car, a massive boulder shifted, trapping Aron's arm under its tremendous weight. For nearly six days, he screamed and violently struggled to free himself as his body shut down from lack of water. Knowing he would soon die of dehydration, Aron was willing to go to any lengths to break free. He used his body weight to break his arm, applied a tourniquet, and amputated, using a dull pocketknife. He literally cut his arm off! When he finished the medieval surgery, he was free![10]

This is how I've felt many times in my spiritual journey. Stuck, helpless, and dying of thirst. Even after we give our lives to Jesus, we sometimes feel trapped by all the things we've done in our past. We've tasted the Living Water we've been looking for, but it seems like the skeletons in our closet are keeping us away from

---

[10] Aron Ralston, *Between a Rock and a Hard Place* (New York, NY: Atria Books, 2004).

the joy we long for. How can we break free from the weight of our sin, past and present? We are forgiven, but how can we be healed?

Murdering Our flesh

In most of the New Testament letters, the first few chapters are devoted to theology (who God is) and doctrine (set of beliefs), but somewhere in the middle of the book is a sudden shift toward the practical. One of these shifts happens in the book of Colossians. After two chapters of eloquent explanation of who Christ is and what the gospel has done on our behalf, Paul says,

> Put to death, therefore, what is earthly in you: sexual immorality, impurity, passion, evil desire, and covetousness, which is idolatry. On account of these the wrath of God is coming. In these you too once walked, when you were living [one version translates this word "addicted"] in them. But now you must put them all away. (Colossians 3:5–8)

Once we've been saved and given a new nature, our lives must be brought in accordance with these spiritual realities. The phrase "put to death" implies a violent attack. Not so much a nice funeral service or a pleasant experience but a ruthless murder. God has given us a new nature. Now we must brutally murder our old desires, thoughts, and actions if we are going to experience the full richness of intimacy with God.

The evidence of our salvation is not just that we prayed a prayer one time or can quote some theological stuff but that it has a lasting impact on our lives. If the prodigal son had stayed in his pigpen quoting how much God loved him and how he'd been saved, he would be gravely mistaken. The proof of his faith was that he left the pigpen and returned home. Genuine faith doesn't stay contained in the heart; it changes our thought patterns and actions, or it's not saving faith. If I went straight back to heroin and never showed any spiritual growth after praying to receive Christ, it would be evidence that I was never truly saved. Martin Luther has been attributed with saying, "We are saved by faith alone, but the faith that saves is never alone."[11] The proof of our salvation is that by the Spirit, we put to death the sin that has gripped us for so long. "Faith without works is dead" (James 2:17).

No Retreat

Jesus tells us to go to extreme measures to put to death our addiction.

> If your right eye causes you to sin, tear it out and throw it away. For it is better that you lose one of your members than that your whole body be thrown into hell. And if your right hand causes you to sin, cut it off and throw it away. For it is better that you lose one of your members than that your whole body go into hell. (Matthew 5:29–30)

Just like Aron Ralston, who cut off his arm to get water, we must be willing to cut anything out of our lives that keeps us from God. This may mean going to a treatment center or detox. For me, this meant moving to another city for a fresh start and being completely abstinent from all drugs and alcohol. Having a drink of alcohol is not sin for a "normal" person, but for us, it is putting a loaded gun in the enemy's hand.

We must follow the example of Cortes, the great Spanish explorer, who upon arriving on the Mexican shore with a vicious battle ahead dismantled all of his ships so there was no turning

---

[11] Martin Luther. *Antidote to the Council of Trent*. 1547.

back. Win the battle or die trying.[12] We also must dismantle all means of retreat into addiction. Phone numbers, relationships, paraphernalia, and everything else. The battle has already been won by Jesus. All we have to do is proceed with courage and complete abandon, never turning back.

Murdering Our Past

To say I had skeletons in my closet when I arrived at rehab would be a vast understatement. Childhood secrets haunted me. Memories of people I robbed, family members I spit on, and sexual sin I committed lingered. I even played a part in others becoming addicted, some of whom have since overdosed and died. I was riddled with fear and shame. Chances are you can relate. A life of addiction brings with it a laundry list of shameful secrets, resentments, and fears.

We have already established that because of the gospel, we are holy and blameless without a spot or blemish. If you are in Christ, Jesus has completely paid for everything you've ever done. God has forgiven you, but we oftentimes have trouble connecting this forgiveness with the darkest spots of our past and extending it to others who have wronged us. The gospel not only brings forgiveness from sin but also deliverance from addiction and freedom from our past. Jesus is the fulfillment of this Old Testament prophecy. "The Spirit of the Lord is upon me, because he has anointed me to proclaim good news to the poor. He has sent me to proclaim liberty to the captives and recovering of sight to the blind, to set at liberty those who are oppressed" (Luke 4:18). Jesus came to bring freedom to those who are oppressed with all kinds of afflictions, especially addiction.

---

[12] Glenn Stanton, "Factchecker: Burning Your Ships For Jesus," The Gospel Coalition, March 13, 2013, https://www.thegospelcoalition.org/article/factchecker-burning-your-ships-for-jesus/.

Slow down as you read the rest of this chapter. It's absolutely crucial you don't just glance over this but you actually launch into action.

Some of my mentors recommended writing down all the things still affecting me from the past so the light of the gospel could shine on each specific situation. In AA and NA, this is called a personal inventory,[13] and in Christian circles, it's called confession. After many hours (over many days) of writing and thinking, I nearly filled an entire notebook. This is one of the most difficult parts of the recovery journey because it digs up so many things that you've kept hidden for years, but temporary discomfort is worth a lifetime of freedom. I went through each skeleton with my mentor, confessing my part, and searched for common threads to learn from them. I even met with people I harmed and asked for their forgiveness. This process gave me more freedom than keeping these things buried would have done. It was like the boulder of my past was being rolled away.

This process of evaluating the past is like having soul surgery. It hurts terribly and there is a long recovery process, but just like having surgery to cut out a cancerous mass, the process is worth the payoff. The pain of not addressing the cancer is much greater than the pain of surgery. Open yourself up to the master surgeon and allow Him to cut out all of the pain, hurt, and sickness. Don't skimp on this part.

We should cry out to God like the psalmist. "Search me, O God, and know my heart! Try me and know my thoughts! And see if there be any grievous way in me, and lead me in the way everlasting" (Psalm 139:23–24)! Take some time to pray this prayer and write down everything from your past that is still

———————————

[13] *Alcoholics Anonymous: The Story of How Many Thousands of Men and Women Have Recovered from Alcoholism.* Fourth ed. New York City: Alcoholics Anonymous World Services, 2001, 59.

affecting you. I'd recommend splitting it up into three categories: sins you've committed, sins done to you, and fears. My mentor had me list what each item on my list affected inside me (emotional security, material security, pride of life, self-esteem, etc.) and what my part was in each of the situations. I found these additions to be very helpful. Dig up the worst of the worst, leaving no secret buried. Again, this is going to be the part you want to skip as you go through this book. But don't! All of the time, effort, and heartache you invest here is going to be well worth it for a lifetime of freedom. The AA book quotes the Oxford Group, which emphasized complete honesty and complete confession, declaring, "Half measures availed us nothing." Write down *everything*, and be *completely* honest.

Bob Hamp, an addiction specialist, says, "Blame is the language of addiction; responsibility is the language of freedom."[14] As you make the list of the sin you've committed, you can accept full responsibility while knowing it's already been paid for. Imagine you are about to go bankrupt for massive debts with many lenders but a wealthy man has agreed to pay all of your debt. You'd have no shame digging up debts small and large from recent days or distant past. Dig up all your debt and submit it all to God. It's already paid for!

The most difficult part for some may be the portion of sins done to us. You may have been abused or experienced some other tragic pain from another person. You have legitimate reason to be upset from these deep wounds, and it will be tempting to hold onto your righteous anger and resentment, but this only hurts you. One of my mentors used to say, "Holding onto resentment is like drinking poison and expecting the other person to die." Mark Driscoll said, "Hell is the place of unforgiveness; when you do not forgive, you are pulling hell up into your life. Heaven is the place

---

[14] Bob Hamp. "Freedom from Addiction" January 9, 2017 in *Bob Hamp*, podcast, https://soundcloud.com/bobhamp/freedom-from-addiction.

of forgiveness; when you forgive, you are inviting heaven down into your life."[15]

Once we understand how much Christ has forgiven us, we will be compelled to forgive others as well. Jesus uses strong language on this topic. "For if you forgive others their trespasses, your heavenly Father will also forgive you, but if you do not forgive others their trespasses, neither will your Father forgive your trespasses." (Matthew 6:14–15)

It may be wise for you to see a Christian counselor to work through deeply rooted issues.

The third and last section was probably the most crucial for me. Fear. I nurtured crippling fear since I was a young child. Putting this down on paper in black and white helped expose the erroneous and irrational nature of many of them. Most of my fears came down to trying to control everything rather than trusting God. Exposing these lies was like flipping a light switch to find the monster in your room was just a shadow of your stuffed animal. God wants us to live lives of deep peace and tranquility. We can trust Him with every aspect of our lives.

Sanctification (the process of becoming more like Jesus) is not an overnight process. It's going to take the rest of our lives. When I went through this process of evaluating and confessing my past, many of the things I had struggled with were instantly healed, but for others, it has been an ongoing process. God does not expect us to be perfect but to run to Him when we mess up. The evidence that you are really following Jesus isn't that you don't struggle with these things anymore but that you live a lifestyle of repentance. This just means that you are running back to God and engaged in the lifelong process of becoming more like Jesus.

As many people have said before, this process gets to the

---

[15] Mark Driscoll, "Demons Transport Bitterness," *Mark Driscoll Ministries (blog)* November 4, 2019, https://markdriscoll.org/demons-transport-bitterness/.

root of our issues rather than merely mowing over them. When I was a child, we lived on a corner lot full of weeds. Crabgrass, dandelions, and many other intruders infected our spacious yard. When we mowed it, it was all the same length and color, masking the infestation for a week or so. Soon the weeds would return, exposing what was beneath the surface. This is what we've done for far too long. We modify our behavior, but we never pull up the roots. God doesn't want you to just look good on the outside. He wants to heal your heart by pulling up sin by the root.

Healing Is Here

When one of my friends was on his way home from elementary school, he jumped off the bus and eagerly ran through the woods. As he neared his house excited to do whatever young boys do after school, a brown recluse spider climbed into his shorts and bit him on the butt. The bump soon became a bruise, but he figured it would just go away like a mosquito bite. As the days passed, he realized it was much more serious, but he didn't want to tell his dad because he was ashamed. He soon found it difficult to even sit down. Finally, the pain got too intense and the consequences so severe that he swallowed his pride, told his dad, and exposed the bite. They went to the hospital, and he was healed within a few days. If he would have waited too much longer, the long-term effects would have been catastrophic.

Maybe you can relate with my buddy's spider bite. Your past is eating you alive, but because of shame, you continue to suffer in silence. David said,

> For when I kept silent, my bones wasted away through my groaning all day long. For day and night your hand was heavy upon me; my strength was dried up as by the heat of summer.

I acknowledged my sin to you, and I did not cover my iniquity; I said, "I will confess my transgressions to the LORD," and you forgave the iniquity of my sin. (Psalm 32:3–5)

You have a really Good Father who loves you and wants to heal you. As many have said before, when we confess our sins to God, we are forgiven, but when we confess our sins to another person, we are healed. "Therefore, confess your sins to one another and pray for one another, that you may be healed. The prayer of a righteous person has great power as it is working" (James 5:16). As you expose your past to yourself, God, and another person, you will find incredible freedom and inexpressible joy.

The gospel has covered us completely; therefore, we can be "naked and unashamed." We have nothing to hide.

Restoration

As we take note of the wreckage of our past, it's easy to feel somewhat hopeless. The dreams that were once bursting in our minds seem dead. Our loved ones want nothing to do with us. The wasteland of our lives seems to absorb any hope into the ashes. It is primarily out of that dark wasteland that God loves to plant the most beautiful gardens of redemption.

> I will restore to you the years
> that the swarming locust has eaten …
> You shall eat in plenty and be satisfied,
> and praise the name of the Lord your God,
> who has dealt wondrously with you. (Joel 2:25, 26)

God will restore to you the years that addiction has eaten. As you search the wasteland of your past and shine light on the darkest places, you'll find God to be more than sufficient. He not only has the authority to remove what's been causing the destruction but also to bring new life that far exceeds our wildest dreams.

Action

1. Make three separate lists: personal sins, sins done to you, and fear (and anything else that affects you that doesn't fit neatly into one of the three categories). Take as much time as you need for this, confessing them to God as you write.
2. Confess these things to your mentor.
3. Make a list of people you are going to make amends with. Begin making these when appropriate.
4. What other practical steps do you need to take to put addiction to death?

CHAPTER 7

Drink Deeply

After six days of tireless struggling, Aron broke free from the boulder by literally cutting off his arm. He climbed down the cliff and staggered toward his car until a group of hikers saw his desperate condition. The first thing he asked them for was not a doctor, food, or even a phone to call home. "Water!" was the first word out of his mouth.[16] In normal conditions, the human body can go three to seven days without water;[17] Aron made it more than six. Our bodies are made up of 60 to 65 percent water, and we need it for digestion, brain activity, joint lubrication, and nearly every other important bodily function. Without it, our bodies shut down.

Just like our bodies can't live without water, our souls can't live without God. When we are separated from Him, our souls begin to fail and life evades us like clinching oil in your fist. Now that we've seen how the gospel deals with the boulder that has

---

[16] Aron Ralston, *Between a Rock and a Hard Place* (New York, NY: Atria Books, 2004).

[17] Dina Spector, "Here's How Many Days a Person Can Survive Without Water," Business Insider, March 8, 2018, https://www.businessinsider.com/how-many-days-can-you-survive-without-water-2014-5.

enslaved us for years, we must learn how to drink what gives us life. We must learn to enjoy God. Just as escaping the boulder was pointless without water on the other side, breaking free from addiction is pointless if we don't drink deeply of God. "As a deer pants for flowing streams, so pants my soul for you, O God. My soul thirsts for God, for the living God" (Psalm 42:1–2).

God is the water our souls are made for. He is where true life is found. For years, we have been drinking the pleasures of this world, hoping to find life and came up empty. We've been drinking the urine of this world, but now we have access to the purest, most satisfying water. You were made to drink Him deeply. "O God, you are my God; earnestly I seek you; my soul thirsts for you; my flesh faints for you, as in a dry and weary land where there is no water" (Psalm 63:1). This access to the presence of God is the main point of the gospel.

"You Will Never Thirst Again"

One hot, summer day, Jesus engaged an adulterous Samaritan woman in a conversation that changed her life forever. She had been married five times and was currently living with a man who wasn't her husband. Because of her shameful past, she went to a well to draw water during the hottest part of the day when no one else was around. After asking her for a drink, Jesus told her:

> Everyone who drinks of this water will be thirsty again, but whoever drinks of the water that I will give him will never be thirsty again. The water that I will give him will become in him a spring of water welling up to eternal life. (John 4:13–14)

Her attempts to quench the thirst of her soul in the beds of many men had fallen short. The real answer to her thirst was not going to be found in another man or more sex but in a relationship with God. Jesus was offering her life—true joy.

He is offering you this same Living Water. Every time we've tried to quench the thirst of our souls with drugs, sex, other people, religion, or the pleasures of this world, we soon became thirsty again, needing more or a stronger drug. But when we taste the presence of God, we will never thirst for anything else again. We've found what we've been looking for the whole time! "Delight yourself in the Lord, and he will give you the desires of your heart" (Psalm 37:4 ESV). He is the desire of your heart, and He is inviting you to make Him the pleasure source of your life.

Be Filled with the Spirit

Many people stop just short of true freedom. They go to treatment, clean out their proverbial house, sweep the floors, make amends, and go to the meetings, but they soon find themselves in a worse state than when they started. I've tearfully watched hundreds of my friends go down this painful path. Jesus said this would happen.

> When the unclean spirit has gone out of a person, it passes through waterless places seeking rest, but finds none. Then it says, "I will return to my house from which I came." And when it comes, it finds the house empty, swept, and put in order. Then it goes and brings with it seven other spirits more evil than itself, and they enter and dwell there, and the last state of that person is worse than the first. So also will it be with this evil generation. (Matthew 12:43–45)

It's not enough to get the bad out; we must also fill the empty space with something—or *someone*. Real freedom is not found in the absence of something (like drugs or alcohol) but in the presence of someone. "Now the Lord is the Spirit, and where the Spirit of the Lord is, there is freedom" (2 Corinthians 3:17). If we are going to experience lasting freedom, we must not only clean our spiritual house as we talked about in the last chapter but must also be filled with the Spirit of God. We must not only pull the weeds but also plant good seeds. Whereas the last chapter was about the pain of soul surgery, this chapter is about experiencing the pleasures of your new life in God.

John the Baptist echoes this truth. "I have baptized you with water, but he [Jesus] will baptize you with the Holy Spirit" (Mark 1:8). Jesus doesn't just want you to be forgiven of sin. He also wants you to be immersed in God. Just like a kid jumping in a refreshing pool on a blazing hot day, God wants you to dive into Him with complete abandon.

As you seek God wholeheartedly, He promises to give Himself to you. "You will seek me and find me, when you seek me with all your heart" (Jeremiah 29:13). "Draw near to God, and he will draw near to you" (James 4:8). God is a Good Father who is happy to fill us with His Spirit.

> And I tell you, ask, and sit will be given to you; seek, and you will find; knock, and it will be opened to you. For everyone who asks receives, and the one who seeks finds, and to the one who knocks it will be opened. What father among you, if his son asks for a fish, will instead of a fish give him a serpent; or if he asks for an egg, will give him a scorpion? If you then, who are evil, know how to give good gifts to your children, how much more will the heavenly Father give the Holy Spirit to those who ask him. (Luke 11:9–13)

God is eager for you to dive into this amazing reality.

Transformation Happens as We Drink

As we drink deeply of God, we will be transformed to be more and more like Jesus.

> And we all, with unveiled face, beholding the glory of the Lord, are being transformed into the same image from one degree of glory to another. For this comes from the Lord who is the Spirit. (2 Corinthians 3:17–18)

As you behold God's beauty, you will be transformed into His image. "Behold" doesn't mean to glance at Him like a stranger passing by but to gaze into His eyes like you're on a date with the love of your life. It means to linger and slowly enjoy Him. This is not like scarfing down fast food but feasting on a filet and savoring every bite. As we feast on His presence like this, our hearts will be more and more transformed and we will live in more and more freedom. We will soon realize our hearts are more in love with God than the old mud pies we once loved so deeply.

The best way to combat addiction or any other sin is to consistently delight yourself in God. Just like a homeless man who hasn't eaten in days will likely eat cat food if it's the only thing available, sin begins to look very appetizing when we haven't feasted on God in a while. But if a well-fed man is offered that same cat food, there is no chance he'd eat the feline chow. He has eaten his fill and has no need for the rubbish. The way to overcome addiction is to feast on a greater joy.

"Walk by the Spirit, and you will not gratify the desires of the flesh" (Galatians 5:16). As we live, led by the Spirit, our lives will show it. We will no longer give into fleshly temptations. We will experience the fruit of the Spirit: "love, joy, peace, patience, kindness, goodness, faithfulness, gentleness, self-control"

(Galatians 5:22–23). This work of God allows us to live in accordance with how He originally designed us to live.

Holiness

Some of my favorite memories with my dad growing up were when he'd take me fishing. We mostly caught common fish, but every once in a while, we'd catch something more exotic. One time we were fishing off the North Carolina coast, and I caught a baby sand shark. It was pretty incredible! As my dad helped reel him in, our family circled around him in amazement as he flailed around our little speedboat. He was at peace in his natural environment in the water, but when we took him out, he violently flailed around like a drowning man. We are very similar with God and His ways. When we are in the presence of God, living according to His will, we are fully alive like a fish in water. But when we begin to live according to our own desires apart from God's perfect design, we feel like a fish out of water. We are desperate for life.

I used to think God's commands were restrictive and killjoys, but now I've realized they are the furthest thing from it. They are the pathway to life. Psalm 16:11 says, "You make known to me the path of life. In your presence is fullness of joy and pleasures forevermore." Every command of God is meant to lead us back into the water—into richer life and greater joy.

In the last chapter, I referenced the shift from theological doctrines to practical in Paul's letter to the church in Colosse. That shift starts with

> If then you have been raised with Christ, seek the things that are above, where Christ is, seated at the right hand of God. Set your minds on things that are above, not on things that are on earth. For you

have died, and your life is hidden with Christ in God. (Colossians 3:1–3)

Jesus is opening your eyes not only to the deadly emptiness of sin and addiction but also to the joy of following His ways. As a result of this, we fix our minds on God and give our bodies over to whatever He says.

As you continue to listen to God and do what He says, you will be able to look back over your spiritual life and realize everything you've done in obedience to God has proven fruitful.

> I appeal to you therefore, brothers, by the mercies of God, to present your bodies as a living sacrifice, holy and acceptable to God, which is your spiritual worship. Do not be conformed to this world, but be transformed by the renewal of your mind, that by testing you may discern what is the will of God, what is good and acceptable and perfect. (Romans 12:1–2)

As I look back over the past nine years of following Jesus, I can clearly see that His will is good, perfect, and pleasing. Every step I've taken in obedience to God has been a step into greater joy!

A Life of Worship

The first time I tasted weed, I became obsessed. My whole life started to revolve around it. I spent most of my time thinking about it, enjoying it, talking about it, or trying to get more of it. I worshipped weed. When I tried Xanax and Klonopin, the same thing happened. I stopped focusing so much on weed because I found a greater pleasure. Once I tried OxyContin, I put down the lesser joys in pursuit of the greater. Heroin had the same effect.

This is how worship works. We center our lives around what we enjoy most, leaving the lesser pleasures behind.

Isaiah 43 gives us a picture of what happens when we taste and see that God is good.

> Remember not the former things, nor consider the things of old. Behold, I am doing a new thing; now it springs forth, do you not perceive it? I will make a way in the wilderness and rivers in the desert. The wild beasts will honor me, the jackals and ostriches, for I give water in the wilderness, rivers in the desert, to give drink to my chosen people, the people whom I formed for myself that they might declare my praise. (verses 18–21)

When the Living Water comes into the wilderness to give drink to the wild animals, they are forever changed and become worshippers of God. When you taste the presence of God, you put down the other mediocre pleasures and center your life on God because He is better. With one sip, we have a new obsession.

This new life of worship affects every aspect of our lives. "So, whether you eat or drink, or whatever you do, do all to the glory of God" (1 Corinthians 10:31). Whether we are eating, drinking, or working, everything can be a response to how amazing He is. Seeing a sunset is no longer just colors in the sky but a glimpse of God's handiwork. The smile of a child becomes a picture of God's happiness. Eating good food no longer is just something we do but stirs our hearts for God's design and goodness. Sex in the context of marriage is no longer just a fleshly fix but becomes worship of a good God who loves you deeply. As we look for God in every aspect of our lives and awe overtakes us, our lives will be filled with more joy than we could ever imagine. We are living how we were created to live: worshipping God. He is the most valuable treasure in the universe and the only One who deserves our worship. He is where the joy is.

Drink More

In Ephesians 5:18, Paul says, "Do not be drunk with wine, for that is debauchery, but instead be filled with the Spirit." God's alternative to addiction to drugs and alcohol is satisfaction in Him. We are not supposed to "just say no" but replace it with something better. The opposite of drunkenness and addiction is not sobriety but being filled with the Holy Spirit. It's not white-knuckled abstinence but being immersed in the joy of knowing God. Some have noted that during the time this verse was written, the wine was so weak that a person would have to drink all day to get drunk. I believe Paul is telling us to pursue God like this. We should drink Him all day every day! It was never enough for us to just have one drink of liquor or one hit from the crack pipe. We went after it with all of our heart, mind, soul, and strength. This is how we should pursue God. "You shall love the LORD your God with all your heart and with all your soul and with all your might" (Deuteronomy 6:5). The other thing to note in Ephesians 5:18 is when we are drunk, we are under the influence of alcohol. We have lost control of our lives and have willingly given control to another. This is what it looks like to be filled with the Holy Spirit. We give ourselves over to the control of God. True freedom is not taking back control of our lives but surrendering that control to God!

Cultural Christianity that is common in the southeastern part of the US, where going to church once a week is enough of the Spirit, is not enough for us. Just like social drinking was never an option for us in our using days, just going to church once a week or half-heartedly following Jesus will not suffice for our deepest longings. Many have tried this form of half-hearted "Christianity" and decided following Jesus doesn't work. I would argue that you have not truly experienced Jesus until you've given your whole heart to Him.

Many times since I started this spiritual journey, I've wondered, *Why was I made like this? Why could I not be a social drinker? Why can't I just be a normal churchgoer? Why do we always need more of God?* John Ortberg responds, "The truth is, the soul's infinite capacity to desire is the mirror image of God's infinite capacity to give. What if the real reason we feel like we never have enough is that God is not yet finished giving? The unlimited neediness of the soul matches the unlimited grace of God."[18]

If you still have a longing in your soul, it means God has more of Himself to give you. Let's drink deeply of Him forever!

Action

1. What are the current ways you are enjoying God?
2. Ask God to fill you with the Holy Spirit and to teach you how to drink deeply of Him.
3. As you read the next chapter, construct a plan of how to pursue God with the same vigor that you pursued alcohol or drugs.

---

[18] John Ortberg, *Soul Keeping: Caring for the Most Important Part of You* (Grand Rapids, MI: Zondervan, 2014).

CHAPTER 8

Training for Joy

Michael Phelps has won more Olympic medals than anyone in the history of the world for his success in swimming. Standing six foot, four, with a wingspan of six foot, seven, and a size fourteen shoe, his physique makes him a natural in the water.[19] His stature is incredible, but what makes him exceptionally elite is his training regimen. He works out thirty to thirty-six hours every week, which includes swimming fifty miles and three days of weightlifting. To maintain these exhausting disciplines, Michael eats 12,000 calories per day—six times the recommended amount for an average adult.[20] This radical training has produced championship results.

By no means is Michael Phelps the perfect example. He struggled when he got distracted and even battled with drugs for a season, but when he trained to win, he saw results. God encourages us to look at the training regimen of athletes like Michael Phelps as examples to follow in our spiritual lives.

---

[19] "Team USA," United States Olympic and Paralympic Committee, https://www.teamusa.org/usa-swimming/athletes/Michael-Phelps.

[20] Richie Allen, "Michael Phelps Workout and Diet," Muscle Prodigy, https://www.muscleprodigy.com/michael-phelps-workout-and-diet/.

> Do you not know that in a race all the runners run,
> but only one receives the prize? So run that you
> may obtain it. Every athlete exercises self-control
> in all things. They do it to receive a perishable
> wreath, but we an imperishable. So I do not run
> aimlessly; I do not box as one beating the air. But
> I discipline my body and keep it under control. (1
> Corinthians 9:24–27)

Most great athletes train in pursuit of medals and fame that will pass away when they do, but we are training for a prize that doesn't fade with time.

The Christian life has massive rewards at the end of our race: Intimacy with God. Eternal life. Infinite joy. Endless pleasure. It is also one that requires ample discipline. If we are going to stay the course and finish the race God has set before us of following Jesus until the end, we will not just be able to coast in neutral; it's going to take discipline. Jocko Willink, a former US Marine, says, "Discipline is the pathway to freedom".[21]

We have already established that we are saved by grace alone through faith alone (Ephesians 2:8–9), but saving faith will always materialize into a life that looks more and more like Jesus. This process is called sanctification, and it takes grace-motivated training. You are a brand-new creation; now it's time to create some brand-new disciplines, rhythms, and habits.

Intimacy Is Not Instant

One of the best examples of what this looks like is marriage.

As the rustic barn doors opened on that chilly January evening, my heart started to pound with great expectation as hundreds of

---

[21] Jocko Willink and Leif Babin, Extreme Ownership: How U.S. Navy Seals Lead and Win (New York, NY: St. Martin's Press, 2015), 274.

our family members and friends turned their heads toward her. My eyes welled up with tears as I saw my gorgeous bride gliding down the aisle. This was the moment we had waited so long for. My life was about to change forever.

We listened intently as the pastor eloquently expounded upon the beautiful meaning of marriage. We read our vows to each other as authentically as a person possibly can with hundreds of people watching and hanging on every word. "I now pronounce you husband and wife. You may kiss the bride." I was elated as we left the venue to begin our new life together.

Immediately, we were in a covenant. Her last name was legally changed, we moved in together, and even our tax status changed. Our position changed instantly, but I've since learned that intimacy is not instant; it takes work. Thousands of married people all over the world are positionally married but living completely separate lives, missing the marital bliss of intimacy.

When you placed your faith in Jesus, you were instantly in an eternal covenant with God. Because of what Jesus has done on your behalf, you are perfect in position with God. Your sin is forgiven and you are a new creation, but the main point of the gospel isn't just right standing with God; it's about intimacy. It's about drinking deeply of Him. This intimacy takes grace-motivated training. Just like how my wife and I must intentionally pursue each other by spending time together, communicating, and going on date nights, God desires us to pursue Him as He pursues us. If you have truly been saved, your position with God will never change, but your intimacy can fluctuate. Just like in marriage, the work to pursue intimacy with God is always worth it.

Spiritual Training

Paul says, "Train yourself for godliness; for while bodily training is of some value, godliness is of value in every way, as it holds promise for the present life and also for the life to come" (1 Timothy 4:7–8). There have been many books written on how to train for godliness, so I will just give a brief summary of six spiritual disciplines that have led me to experience more joy in God, rather than giving an exhaustive list. Applying these training exercises in your daily life will grow you in godliness and allow you to experience more joy in God.

Prayer

One of the first things I experienced after arriving at rehab was prayer. We started and ended most meetings with the Serenity Prayer or the Lord's Prayer. We quickly learned to recite these without any effort, but most of us rarely thought about what we were saying or who we were talking to. Some of my mentors encouraged me to spend time praying every morning and every night, so I began hitting my knees right when I woke up and right before closing my eyes at night. This was when I really began to contemplate the real purpose of prayer and experience the benefits.

Prayer is simply talking to God. Jesus teaches us to view Him as our Daddy when we pray, "Our Father ..." Rather than reciting empty phrases, prayer is an intimate conversation with a close friend who never gets tired of us. God actually encourages us to pray all the time (1 Thessalonians 5:17). This doesn't have to be a well-structured, eloquent discourse but a real conversation with a real God who is eager to hear from you, His child.

Just how my marriage would be cold and distant if I never spoke to my wife, our relationship with God will grow cold if we never speak to Him from our hearts. When my wife and I communicate regularly and talk about everything, we feel closer and our love for each other grows. As we learn to come to God to just talk, listen, adore, intercede, thank, and ask, we will find our hearts growing more in love with Him and we will experience greater depths of freedom.

Not only do we fall more in love with Him, but He also actually answers us when we pray.

> If you abide in me, and my words abide in you,
> ask whatever you wish, and it will be done for
> you ... These things I have spoken to you, that my
> joy may be in you, and that your joy may be full.
> (John 15:7, 11)

When we pray, things actually change, including us. Jesus is inviting us to get alone and begin training for more joy by spending time with God in prayer.

Bible

When one of my first mentors recommended I begin reading the Bible, I never thought it would become one of the sweetest treasures in my life. I viewed the Bible as an outdated book without relevance in today's world. As I began reading it on a regular basis, I found myself not just reading words on a page but communing with God. Bill Johnson often says, "The Bible is Jesus in print. Don't tell me you love Jesus if you don't love His Word."[22]

Just as prayer is the way to talk to God, the Bible is one of the main ways God talks to us.

> All Scripture is breathed out by God and profitable
> for teaching, for reproof, for correction, and for
> training in righteousness, that the man of God

---

[22] Bill Johnson, The Way of Life: Experiencing The Culture of Heaven on Earth (Shippensburg, PA: Destiny Image Publishers, 2018),142.

may be complete, equipped for every good work.
(2 Timothy 3:16–17)

The Bible is literally God's Words to us. God spoke the universe into existence by His Word, and it still holds that much power today.

> For the word of God is living and active, sharper than any two-edged sword, piercing to the division of soul and of spirit, of joints and of marrow, and discerning the thoughts and intentions of the heart. (Hebrews 4:12)

As we read it, we experience His life and breath into our souls.

I've learned to love it like King David.

> The law of the Lord is perfect,
> reviving the soul;
> the testimony of the Lord is sure,
> making wise the simple;
> the precepts of the Lord are right,
> rejoicing the heart;
> the commandment of the Lord is pure,
> enlightening the eyes;
> the fear of the Lord is clean,
> enduring forever;
> the rules of the Lord are true,
> and righteous altogether.
> More to be desired are they than gold,
> even much fine gold;
> sweeter also than honey
> and drippings of the honeycomb. (Psalm 19:7–10)

David viewed the Word of God as more valuable than millions of dollars and sweeter than his favorite dessert. We should approach it with this same value. Matt Chandler encourages, "Don't read the Bible likes it's an old newspaper; read it like you're on a date!" (Chandler 2018) Enjoy it. As we discipline ourselves to spend intentional time reading and meditating on God's Word every day, we will find our minds being renewed and our souls being refreshed, and we'll have a clearer understanding of the narrow pathway that leads to life. This may be the most essential training exercise of all.

Gratitude

A few months into my freedom journey, I heard a message on the topic of gratitude that radically transformed my life. The speaker pointed to the Bible passage that teaches that gratitude is the pathway to the presence of God. "Enter his gates with thanksgiving, and his courts with praise! Give thanks to him; bless his name!" (Psalm 100:4). From that point on, whenever I was feeling ungrateful and irritable, I would write a gratitude list. As I wrote, I thanked God for each of the underserved blessings in my life, and joy filled my heart. Rather than saying, "I *have to* go to work today," I started saying, "I *get to* go to work today." This small mind-set shift changed my perspective in every aspect of life. This discipline is a constant fight but is one of the most powerful tools that remains in my tool belt to this day.

Private Worship

Throughout Christian history, one of the main ways people have experienced God is through singing. "Make a joyful noise to the Lord, all the earth! Serve the Lord with gladness! Come into his presence with singing" (Psalm 100:1–2)! We obviously do this regularly when we gather with other Christians at church services, but I also love worshipping God in private. My voice is pretty terrible, but there is something very intimate about singing loudly to God when no one else is around. Genuine worship has immense power.

In Acts 16, after Paul and Silas were put in prison for casting a demon out of a slave girl, they began to pray and sing in their jail cell. "Suddenly there was a great earthquake, so that the foundations of the prison were shaken. And immediately all the doors were opened, and everyone's bonds were unfastened" (verse 26). Not only do we get to experience God when we sing, but the chains of our addiction are broken when we worship God in private. Make it a discipline to sing to God with all your heart in the best of times and the worst of times.

Nightly Review

Just as a professional athlete and his coach regularly evaluate the effectiveness of the training regimen in order to continually get better, we must also regularly evaluate each day to continue to improve. Many Christians in history have implemented something called an "examen." Alcoholics Anonymous encourages a version of this.

> When we retire at night, we constructively review our day. Were we resentful, selfish, dishonest, or afraid? Do we owe an apology? Have we kept something to ourselves which should be discussed with another person at once? Were we kind and loving toward all? What could we have done better? Were we thinking of ourselves most of the time? Or were we thinking of what we could do for others, of what we could pack into the stream of life? But we must be careful not to drift into worry,

remorse, or morbid reflection, for that would diminish our usefulness to others. After making our review we ask God's forgiveness and inquire what corrective measures should be taken.[23]

I also have a version of this nightly review I have put together from many sources and things that I need to review based on my natural bents and personal struggles. This has gone through many revisions, but this is the current format:

Part 1- Gratitude

- Acknowledge/invite the Holy Spirit.
- Review the day and give thanks for specifics.

Part 2- Reflect

- Did I abide in Jesus today?
- How did I show love to my wife today? Did I speak life?
- Was I fearful? "Do not fear for I AM with you." (Isaiah 41:10)
- Was I focused on me or God and others?
- How did I seek to advance God's kingdom today?
- Was I on my phone too much?
- Who did I encourage today?

Part 3- Repent

- What do I need to ask forgiveness for?
- Do I need to talk to anyone or make amends?
- Did I agree with anything contrary to the fruit of the Spirit (love, joy, peace, patience, etc.)?

---

[23] *Alcoholics Anonymous: The Story of How Many Thousands of Men and Women Have Recovered from Alcoholism.* Fourth ed. (New York City: Alcoholics Anonymous World Services, 2001), 86.

Part 4- Remember

- Remember Jesus's words "It is finished" and the implications of the gospel.
- Remember my identity as a beloved son of God. "He gives His beloved sleep" (Psalm 127:2).
- Ask Him to speak to you as you sleep.

This discipline allows us to continually get better and clean up the wreckage of that day, rather than allowing it to build up. It's like cleaning your house. When my wife and I take fifteen minutes to clean up after dinner and straighten up the house after our company leaves, the house is typically is pretty good shape. But if we begin slacking on this small discipline, our house soon becomes a pigsty in which we must spend a few whole days putting it back together. In our spiritual lives, fifteen minutes each night will save you from much pain in the future.

Fasting

This is the most hated spiritual discipline of many, but is one of the most fruitful, especially for people with a past in addiction. Fasting is abstaining from food or some other comfort in order to experience more of God or to hear clearly from God. Every three months, my wife and I take an overnight trip that we call our quarterly getaway. We typically turn off our phones and remove distractions so we can connect, communicate, and experience greater intimacy. This is what fasting does for us spiritually. It removes certain comforts so we can focus more fully on God and experience drink more deeply of Him.

There are many examples of this in the Bible and many ways to do it. Daniel fasted from meat and other delicacies, eating mainly fruit, vegetables, and whole grains for twenty-one days. This

"Daniel fast" is still very common today. Jesus fasted for forty days from both food and water. I would not recommend this type of fast unless approved by a doctor and pastor. Many people do a weekly fast whereby they abstain from eating two meals back to back one day per week. Fasting from social media, TV, or caffeine is also very common. The length and type of fast doesn't matter as much as the heart behind it and what you fill the time with that you'd normally be eating or doing the activity you are abstaining from.

Fasting is a beautiful gift from God to help experience more of His presence. It has also been noted in the medical community that fasting has a profound impact on the brain and has been known to help break addictions.

In Secret

There are many other spiritual disciplines we could go into great depth on—silence and solitude, sabbath, and many more—but the six aforementioned are a great place to start. Jesus says you should do these in secret, trusting that God will reward you. It's been said, "Who you are when nobody's looking is who you really are." If you fill the secret places of your life with devotion to Jesus, the public parts of your life will follow suit. By God's grace, chase after these spiritual disciplines with the intensity that you pursued drugs and alcohol, and you will find your heart, mind, and body changing to look more like Jesus.

Physical Training

Not all helpful habits are overtly spiritual in nature. Omar Manejwala, one of the nation's experts in addiction, notes that forming new habits and routines actually changes the brain and helps us to live in lasting freedom. "Habits are not forgotten, but replaced. Think of habits as recordings on magnetic tape. The only way to remove them is to write over them."[24] To rewire our brains from destructive habits, we must create new ones that line up with our new lives. God designed our brains to literally heal themselves over time! I've found the following physical disciplines to be a valuable aspect of my freedom journey.

Find a Rhythm

Before I started following Jesus, my life was chaos. The only real routine I had was my work schedule (if I decided to show up). I went to bed in the middle of the night and woke up whenever felt right, oftentimes late in the afternoon. One of the first things I noticed after arriving at treatment was how rigid they were about our schedule. Morning meditation and breakfast were at 6 a.m. There were meetings all day: 8:30 a.m., 12 p.m., 5 p.m., 8 p.m., etc. At first, I resented this structure, but eventually I saw its value. I have remained fairly disciplined in this area to this day. My wife makes fun of me because I put literally everything on my Google Calendar, from meetings to date night and even bedtime. Rhythm and order are not the source of our recovery, but they are useful tools God uses to restore us.

In the first book of the Bible, we see God designed the world to work with a rhythm. As God created the universe and filled the earth, He changed formlessness and chaos into order and rhythm.

> The earth was without form and void, and darkness was over the face of the deep. And the Spirit of God was hovering over the face of the waters. And God said, "Let there be light," and there was light. And God saw that the light was good. And God

---

[24] Omar Manejwala, *Craving: Why We Can't Seem to Get Enough* (Center City, MN: Hazelden, 2013). 148-149.

separated the light from the darkness. God called the light Day, and the darkness he called Night. And there was evening and there was morning, the first day. (Genesis 1:2–5)

We were created to operate with rhythm and order; without it, we do not flourish. I believe God wants to restore order in your schedule to help restore order in all aspects of your life.

Care for Your Body

There is no lack of data to show the impact a healthy body has on the brain, but research also shows it positively impacts recovery from addiction. Our bodies are God's temple, and we are called to steward them well. Although God doesn't demand we all become world-class athletes, He does say, "Physical training is of some value." Three disciplines that I've adopted into my life are regular exercise, eating healthy, and a good night's sleep.

Exercise has been known to reduce stress, increase energy levels, improve mood, and even protect the brain from the negative impacts of long-term drug.[25] As I've started doing CrossFit a few times a week, I have experienced all of these benefits. Pick something that you might enjoy and do it on a regular basis: walking, basketball, lifting weights, swimming, running, etc. Exercise is not the ultimate fix and cannot become our god, but it does have its benefits.

Nutrition has also been proven to help the recovery process.[26] When I was in active addiction, my diet consisted mainly of sweet tarts, raspberry lemonade, and handfuls of pills. When I arrived at

---

[25] "Exercise and Addiction Recovery: 7 Benefits," Futures Recovery Healthcare, October 25, 2018. https://futuresrecoveryhealthcare.com/knowledge-center/exercise-and-addiction-recovery-7-benefits/.

[26] "Substance Use Recovery and Diet," Medline Plus, accessed July 22, 2020, https://medlineplus.gov/ency/article/002149.htm.

treatment, I was extremely malnourished, weighing a whopping one hundred pounds. I didn't know the science behind it at the time, but as I started eating healthier, I started feeling better. One article states,

> Nutrients give the body energy, help build and repair organ tissue, and strengthen the immune system ... Nutrition also plays an important role in mood. Research suggests that changes in your diet can alter brain structure both chemically and physiologically, and influence your behavior. Furthermore, the consumption of certain foods has been tied to increased production of key neurotransmitters like serotonin.[27]

Not only do exercise and nutrition help support us in this journey, but a recent study by Penn State University shows that getting a good night's sleep is also linked to lasting recovery from addiction.[28] Better sleep helps people stay sober. God gives us sleep as a good gift to bring healing to our bodies, minds, and souls, "He gives His beloved sleep" (Psalm 127:2). Isn't that good news?

Partnering with God

By themselves, none of these disciplines mean anything. We are only justified by God's grace, and we are only truly freed from

---

[27] Jenny Smiechowski, "Nutrition and Addiction Recovery: How Healthy Eating Can Help You Stay Sober," The Fix, April 5, 2014, https://www. thefix.com/content/nutrition-and-addiction-recovery-how-healthy-eating-can-help-you-stay-sober?page=all.

[28] Kristie Auman-Bauer, "Sleep Quality and Emotions Affect Opioid Addiction Recovery," Penn State News, Penn State, January 4, 2017, https://news.psu.edu/story/443476/2017/01/04/sleep-quality-and-emotions-affect-opioid-addiction-recovery.

addiction by the gospel. Our primary focus in growing in our relationship with God is Him changing our hearts, but we must also train for godliness through spiritual and physical disciplines. As we give ourselves over to prayer, reading the Bible, fighting for gratitude, worshiping God in private, nightly reviews, fasting, and a healthy lifestyle, we are partnering with God in this holistic transformation.

No one is able to casually follow Jesus and finish the race without great measures of discipline, but for the person who has struggled with addiction, this is even more true. Just like a diabetic must be much more disciplined with sugar consumption and formerly obese people must be disciplined in their exercise and eating, we must be more disciplined in our training for godliness. God is not calling you to a mediocre spiritual life; He is calling you to live the abundant life of Christ. It's the full, rich life available to those who embrace discipline. Those who do live a championship life.

The late Jim Rohn famously said, "We must all suffer from one of two pains: the pain of discipline or the pain of regret. The difference is discipline weighs ounces while regret weighs tons." Every person has this choice. Will we discipline ourselves today and experience the benefits, or will we punt on the pain of today surely to reap impending remorse in the future? I have looked many drug addicts in their eyes as they tearfully experience this throbbing regret. They knew the right way to go but chose not to embrace the pain of discipline. After losing everything, including their families, once again, the pain is so tangible I can feel it too. Don't let this be your story. Fully surrender everything to Jesus, and live a life full of trust and training. Let's run this race with discipline, knowing the eternal prize of endless joy is ours for the taking.

Action

1. What time(s) each day are you going to spend focused time reading the Bible and praying? (The book of John is a great place to start.)
2. How can you begin to implement the other spiritual disciplines listed in this chapter?
3. What planner or online calendar will you use to begin ordering your life?
4. What adjustments do you need to make to your eating, exercise, and sleeping habits?

CHAPTER 9

Wild Mission

In the early 1500s, a Polish astronomer named Nicolaus Copernicus discovered we are not at the center of the universe. Up until this revelation, the widely accepted view was the earth was the center of the solar system and everything orbited around it. What is now known as the Copernican Revolution was the groundbreaking realization that the sun is actually the center and everything, including us, revolves around it.[29] This discovery changed our world forever. We had a new center.

When Jesus saves us, He begins doing a similar work in our hearts. I used to be at the center of my own universe and expected everyone to revolve around me, including God. My opinion is what mattered. Everyone and everything were created to meet my needs and serve me. This is the mind-set of most people, especially people in addiction. The truth is God does not revolve around us like some sort of deified butler; we revolve around Him. People are not here to meet our needs; we're here to serve them and point them to the real center. I am not the crown jewel of the universe; God is.

---

[29] Robert S. Westman, *Encyclopedia Britannica*, s.v. "Nicolaus Copernicus," accessed July 22, 2020, https://www.britannica.com/biography/Nicolaus-Copernicus#ref404946.

When this miracle happens, everything begins to shift and we reap the benefits. Our joy is multiplied when Jesus takes His rightful seat at the center of our universe. John Ortberg observed,

> An addict is the supreme example of trying to satisfy the soul with all the wrong things. The more it's fed, the more it craves ... We were wired for ecstasy. Not the drug, but pure ecstatic joy. Our ceaseless craving for more, though it can kill us when unredeemed, may be a hint of the joy that we were made for when the soul finds its center in God. The paradox of soul satisfaction is this: When I die to myself, my soul comes alive.[30]

Selfishness versus Selflessness

Self-centeredness is the antithesis of joy in God. When we are consumed with ourselves, we're miserable, but when we die to ourselves and God becomes our new center, we come alive. Jesus said this in many different ways.

> Truly, truly, I say to you, unless a grain of wheat falls into the earth and dies, it remains alone; but if it dies, it bears much fruit. Whoever loves his life loses it, and whoever hates his life in this world will keep it for eternal life. (John 12:24–25)

> If anyone would come after me, let him deny himself and take up his cross and follow me. For whoever would save his life will lose it, but whoever loses his life for my sake will find it. For

---

[30] John Ortberg, *Soul Keeping: Caring for the Most Important Part of You* (Grand Rapids, MI: Zondervan, 2014).

> what will it profit a man if he gains the whole
> world and forfeits his soul? Or what shall a man
> give in return for his soul? (Matthew 16:24–26)

Rather than expecting people to serve us, we are called to give up our lives for the good of others. Rather than being served and miserable, we're called to serve others out of an overflow of joy in God. Paul points to Jesus as the ultimate example.

> Do nothing from selfish ambition or conceit, but
> in humility count others more significant than
> yourselves. Let each of you look not only to his
> own interests, but also to the interests of others.
> Have this mind among yourselves, which is yours
> in Christ Jesus, who, though he was in the form of
> God, did not count equality with God a thing to be
> grasped, but emptied himself, by taking the form
> of a servant, being born in the likeness of men.
> And being found in human form, he humbled
> himself by becoming obedient to the point of
> death, even death on a cross. (Philippians 2:3–8)

The antidote to a miserable, selfish life is selflessness that flows from a heart that has been transformed by the gospel. The most pleasurable life is one lived for the fame of God and the good of others. Jesus laid down his life "for the joy set before Him" (Hebrews 12:2), and we are called to do the same.

Early in my freedom journey, a young homeless man with mental health issues and alcoholism came into my life. He was fairly annoying and most everyone had written him off after countless vain attempts to help. His social skills felt like nails on a chalkboard. I believe God sent him to teach me this vivifying concept.

I spent countless hours with him, hearing about his past

and sharing how he could know God and break free from his alcoholism. There were many times when I was dreading spending time with him, but afterward, I was filled with such a pure joy that I sat in solitude hoping not to scare it away. The love of God was more real in those moments than nearly any other time in my life.

I've since become addicted to the joy that serving people brings to my soul. There are times I feel like it and many when I don't, but I do it anyway, knowing the sweet joy waiting on the other side of selfless service. Jesus encouraged this. "Truly, I say to you, as you did it to one of the least of these my brothers, you did it to me" (Matthew 25:40). Serving people who aren't able to return the favor is equivalent to serving Jesus. When we get out of ourselves by serving others, we align ourselves with Jesus and feel His rich presence. This is the essence of love.

Love Others

When Jesus was asked about the greatest commandment, He said,

> You shall love the Lord your God with all your heart and with all your soul and with all your mind. This is the great and first commandment. And a second is like it: You shall love your neighbor as yourself. (Matthew 22:37–39)

Without this love, all of our serving others is pointless. "If I give away all I have, and if I deliver up my body to be burned, but have not love, I gain nothing" (1 Corinthians 13:3). That's a pretty radical verse. Paul says if we become martyrs but don't have love in our hearts, it is pointless. Where does this love come from?

> Beloved, let us love one another, for love is from God, and whoever loves has been born of God and

knows God. Anyone who does not love does not
know God, because God is love ... Beloved, if God
so loved us, we also ought to love one another. (1
John 4:7–8; 11)

Genuine love comes from a clear understanding and real experience of God's love for us in the gospel. Once we experience His incredible love, we will want to do the same for others. "For the love of Christ controls us" (2 Corinthians 5:14). This is what it looks like to revolve around Jesus. We are so enamored by God's love that we give up our lives to serve others, and in doing so, we are filled with holy joy. This can look like holding a door for someone, giving money to the poor, letting someone stay with you for a season, or giving someone a ride. It could look like starting a nonprofit to feed the poor, care for orphans, save people from the sex slave industry, or help others find freedom from addiction. It could mean being a missionary, planting a church, or doing thousands of other things, but the pinnacle of this love is sharing the best gift: the gospel.

Don't Hide the Antidote

I heard a preacher tell the following story one time, and it made a profound impact on my life: Imagine everyone in the world is in one massive hospital suffering from cancer, with differing levels of severity. Yours is a very progressive form and you are nearing death. As your breathing starts to slow and your heartbeat weakens, a man walks in the hospital room and asks, "Do you want to get well?"

What a stupid question. Of course, I don't want to die. "What do you mean?" you say.

He explains how he'd been afflicted with the same form of cancer but was given an antidote that made him well. He offers it to you.

It's worth a shot. After taking the medicine, your heartbeat quickens and your breathing regulates. It's a miracle! With tears streaming down your face, you jump up and give the man a massive hug. You have been made well!

Before leaving the room, he has one more gift. "I am also going to leave you with an unlimited supply of the antidote you can share with anyone you wish. Go and help other people like you."

This is a picture of our current reality. Everyone in the world is afflicted with the progressive disease of sin, all with different symptoms. At some point in your life, someone shared the gospel with you and you were brought back to life, forgiven, and healed. You now possess an unlimited supply of the cure and have been commanded to share it with as many other people as possible.

Rather than continuing to lie in bed like we're still sick or only hanging out with other healed people while our suitcases full of the antidote collect dust in the corner, we are called to go room to room offering dying people the only thing that can make them well. There is a hospital full of people on the brink of death and eternal punishment. It's our responsibility and joy to share it with everyone.

Jesus commands us, "Go into all the world and proclaim the gospel to the whole creation. Whoever believes and is baptized will be saved, but whoever does not believe will be condemned" (Mark 16:15–16). Once we've experienced the grace and love of God in salvation, we are not only saved, satisfied, and set free but also sent on a mission to bring the kingdom of God to earth and tell others about how they can be saved too. Our purpose is to enjoy God and share Him with as many people as possible. You have an unlimited supply of the antidote that is sufficient for reaching the world.

There are many examples in the Bible and in history of people like you and me who took this command seriously and saw many lives changed.

"One Thing I Do Know …"

A blind man once approached Jesus, asking to be healed. Jesus spit on the ground, made mud from the saliva, and put it on the man's eyes. (Clearly, Jesus works in mysterious ways.) He told him to go wash in a certain pool, and the man came back seeing! The formerly blind man began sharing his story and was hammered with hundreds of questions about how he was healed and who Jesus is.

> So they said to him, "Then how were your eyes opened?" He answered, "The man called Jesus made mud and anointed my eyes and said to me, 'Go to Siloam and wash.' So I went and washed and received my sight." (John 9:10–11)

> So the Pharisees again asked him how he had received his sight. And he said to them, "He put mud on my eyes, and I washed, and I see." (verse 15)

> So for the second time they called the man who had been blind and said to him, "Give glory to God. We know that this man [meaning Jesus] is a sinner." He answered, "Whether he is a sinner I do not know. **One thing I do know**, that though I was blind, now I see." (verses 24–25; emphasis mine)

The man didn't know much theology or apologetics, but he'd encountered Jesus and was compelled to tell everyone what happened. People can argue with our theology, but they can't argue with our story. We don't need to know everything; we just need to know. "I was blind, but now I see."

Of course, we should grow in our knowledge and understanding of God and the Bible over time, but we can't let lack of knowledge hinder us from obeying God's command to go and tell others. Even the early apostles didn't know everything. "Now when they saw the boldness of Peter and John, and perceived that they were uneducated, common men, they were astonished. And they recognized that they had been with Jesus" (Acts 4:13). A more literal translation is "unschooled, ordinary idiots," who were equipped to flip the world upside down with the message of Jesus because they had spent time with Jesus. If you have a story and have spent time with Jesus, you are equipped to begin sharing what He's done in your life.

Don't be ashamed of your story. God has given us messy stories to show His great power. I have been sharing my story since I got saved, and it has been a tool God is using to lead many to salvation. All we need to know to start is this: "I was enslaved, but now I'm free. Jesus did it."

How?

There are many practical ways of serving others and advancing the gospel. Praying for people is a great place to start. Build relationships with lost people, have them over for dinner, and serve them by meeting practical needs. Invite them to church, tell them your story, and share the gospel. It's amazing what God will do as you step out in faith.

Shortly after I gave my life to Jesus, I started working as a lifeguard and swim coach at our local YMCA. It was a very small, slightly outdated facility, but each day dozens of people would come to swim in the four-lane pool. I made it my aim to share my story with nearly every person who walked through those doors. I invited many other lifeguards to church and saw many come to know Christ. Right before I moved away, I sent an email out to all of the swim team parents, explaining the reason for us winning the Florence Summer Swim League Championship (I know: impressive) was because of Jesus. I shared my story and explained how they too could be saved. God used that fresh fire to inspire others but also to build my confidence for a lifetime of sharing the gospel.

When Jesus called me to begin sharing the gospel, I was extremely scared and felt extremely inadequate due to my speech impediment. I could barely order a hamburger or hold a conversation. I reluctantly agreed and have seen God move in more ways than I ever imagined. He began slowly healing my speech and using my weakness to show His power. Sometimes it would go well, and other times it wouldn't. Since then, God has opened up countless doors and allows me to travel around the world telling my story, sharing the gospel, and seeing thousands of lives transformed. What is God calling you to do?

The reason I tell you this isn't to brag about how many people I've told about Jesus but to encourage you to begin sharing your faith with everyone God has placed in your life. The places you work, live, and spend time are opportunities for you to share the antidote! You can do this wherever you are, even if you are currently incarcerated. Make it your aim to love, serve, and share the gospel with everyone God has placed in your life. You will be amazed at what He does.

Jesus doesn't only command us to make converts but also to make disciples.

> All authority in heaven and on earth has been given to me. Go therefore and make disciples of all nations, baptizing them in the name of the Father and of the Son and of the Holy Spirit, teaching them to observe all that I have commanded you. And behold, I am with you always, to the end of the age. (Matthew 28:18–20)

Once a person places their faith in Jesus, you can baptize them and then teach them how to obey everything Jesus taught.

This is a messy, lifelong process, but it's worth it every time. Truly surrendering to Jesus as Lord and center of your life means you make this commission the purpose of your life. God may even call you to plant a church, start a recovery center, or do something else on a full-time basis.

We are not on this journey alone. Right before Jesus ascended into heaven, He promised the disciples, "But you will receive power when the Holy Spirit has come upon you, and you will be my witnesses in Jerusalem and in all Judea and Samaria, and to the end of the earth" (Acts 1:8). A few days later, that promise came true. While those same disciples are praying, the Holy Spirit fell on them and empowered them to go share the antidote with the known world. Many of them ended up being killed for their message, but not before thousands were set free by it. This same power is the one that raised Jesus from the dead and is inside you. As you give up your life to serve others and share Jesus with them, the Holy Spirit will empower you and fill you with overflowing joy.

Mission Is Good but Not God

This new purpose and calling should be a big part of our lives, but it cannot become the center or else we have just traded one addiction for another. God must remain at the center of our existence, and serving others and advancing the gospel must flow out of that relationship. George Mueller said,

> Above all things see to it that your souls are happy in the Lord. Other things may press upon you, the Lord's work may even have urgent claims upon your attention, but I deliberately repeat, it is of supreme and paramount importance that you should seek above all things to have your souls truly happy in God Himself! Day by day seek to

make this the most important business of your life.[31]

Mueller was a man who accomplished miraculous things for the kingdom of God and helped many people, but Jesus remained central.

Jesus also emphasized this. "I am the vine; you are the branches. Whoever abides in me and I in him, he it is that bears much fruit, for apart from me you can do nothing" (John 15:5). Many pastors and other Christians have made ministry the center of their universe and have found themselves eventually empty and fruitless. Serving others and loving people are two planets that orbit God, but they cannot take His place. Fruitful ministry flows out of intimacy with God. Make it your first priority to be connected to Jesus, and then let that flow into service, genuine love, and zeal to reach the world with the message of Jesus.

Stay Wild

When my wife was younger, she always wanted a peacock as a pet. She jokingly said she'd marry the first guy who bought her one. I wanted to be that guy! After a few months of dating, I began my search to find a pet peacock to win her hand in marriage. After a while, I found one on Craigslist for $100. I called the owner immediately and told him I was on the way to pick it up, without asking many questions.

Upon arriving, I realized this was not a trained pet. Although he was incredibly beautiful, he was wild. The man had caught him a few days prior and I was the sucker giving him $100 for a wild animal. It was fully grown and had a wingspan of nearly five feet. He paced back and forth in the pen and nearly clawed us to death

---

[31] George Mueller, *A Narrative of Some of the Lord's Dealings with George Mueller* (Muskegon, MI: Dust and Ashes Publications, 2003).

as we put him in a kennel to transport him. The entire drive home, he smacked his head on the top of the cage, sounding like rocks were being thrown at my car.

My then girlfriend was overjoyed to own her dream pet but soon realized he was not what she expected. She couldn't hold him, play with him, or really do anything but watch him pace back and forth. Within a few weeks, Sherman (classic name for a peacock) escaped back into the wild where he belonged.

God's heart for wild people, like you and me, is not to domesticate us to hide in a church building for the rest of our lives; His heart is to transform our hearts and unleash us in wild worship of Jesus and wild mission for the kingdom. One reason many new believers with a wild past are frustrated is due to well-meaning Christians attempting to domesticate them rather than unleash them. God doesn't want a lion to become a house cat; He wants to unleash us back into the wilderness as new creations to do wild work for the kingdom.

Jesus is still speaking, "Go ..."

You have a new center.

Action

1. Who is at the center of your universe? How can you make Jesus the center?
2. How can you begin serving and loving others today?
3. Who can you share your story and the gospel with today?
4. What would it look like for you to devote the rest of your life to wild mission? Spend some time in prayer, asking God to use you to change the world.

CHAPTER 10

How to Never Relapse

I literally got arrested on my honeymoon.

My wife and I were coming back from our dream vacation in Punta Cana, eager to begin our new life together. We were still on our honeymoon high, giggling and flirting as we waited in the customs line. This joy soon turned to sober fear.

The agent put us in a small room with only a few others and told us we couldn't use our cell phones. An hour later, I was called up to the counter and told I had an active arrest warrant from my addiction days. I broke the news to my new wife, who I'm sure was wondering what kind of man she had married. They handcuffed me and took me to a small holding cell, where they searched and questioned me. They even took my shoestrings!

Four hours later, they transported me to jail. When we arrived, the corrections officers made us aware the warrant had been taken care of years ago and they released me back to my beautiful bride.

This is oftentimes how our past works. It pops up at the most random times and lands us where we never thought we'd be: back in those familiar handcuffs.

I've seen this happen far too often in many friends' lives. After weeks, months, or even years of sobriety, they end up enslaved again—cuffed to their vomit. Leaving the holiday at sea, they return to the mud pies in the slum. Many have even died, thinking they can still handle their normal dose but their tolerance had diminished.

Many addiction specialists have declared that relapse is part of the recovery process. The graves of thousands have taken their advice, but it doesn't have to be that way. Many have been set free for good, never to return to their ex-lover. The holiday at sea has become their eternal home. How can this be your reality? How can you have complete freedom forever? How can you have lasting joy?

Jesus sheds some light on this in Luke 8:4–8, in the parable of the sower.

> And when a great crowd was gathering and people from town after town came to him, he said in a parable, "A sower went out to sow his seed. And as he sowed, some fell along the path and was trampled underfoot, and the birds of the air devoured it. And some fell on the rock, and as it grew up, it withered away, because it had no moisture. And some fell among thorns, and the thorns grew up with it and choked it. And some fell into good soil and grew and yielded a hundredfold." As he said these things, he called out, "He who has ears to hear, let him hear."

Jesus then explains this parable to His disciples.

> Now the parable is this: The seed is the word of God. The ones along the path are those who have heard; then the devil comes and takes away

the word from their hearts, so that they may not believe and be saved. And the ones on the rock are those who, when they hear the word, receive it with joy. But these have no root; they believe for a while, and in time of testing fall away. And as for what fell among the thorns, they are those who hear, but as they go on their way they are choked by the cares and riches and pleasures of life, and their fruit does not mature. As for that in the good soil, they are those who, hearing the word, hold it fast in an honest and good heart, and bear fruit with patience. (verses 11–15)

In this parable, Jesus shows us the spiritual journey of four different types of people. Three of them fall away, but one perseveres until the end. These examples shed light on some of the main pitfalls we need to watch out for and give us hope and show us the pathway to remain faithful and free forever.

Pitfall 1- The Devil

The first pitfall Jesus tells us to watch out for is demonic opposition. In the parable, the devil prevents the hearer from ever believing, but he is a continued antagonist for the believer. We see this in Genesis 3 when Adam and Eve are tempted in the garden of Eden. Satan comes to the woman, as the man stands by passively, and questions what God said. This is his main tactic. He will twist and question what God has clearly said so you will turn away from following Jesus and return to what you know leads to death. "Did God actually say …? You will not surely die. God is holding out on you." His tactics have not changed. "Did God actually say you shouldn't get high? You won't surely die if you get high or drunk just one more time. God is holding out on you by not letting you feel good." He has destroyed millions by these lies.

Peter warns us, "Be sober-minded; be watchful. Your adversary the devil prowls around like a roaring lion, seeking someone to devour" (1 Peter 5:8). Paul does too.

> Put on the whole armor of God, that you may be able to stand against the schemes of the devil. For we do not wrestle against flesh and blood, but against the rulers, against the authorities, against the cosmic powers over this present darkness, against the spiritual forces of evil in the heavenly places. (Ephesians 6:11–12)

We have a real spiritual enemy who wants to steal, kill, and destroy everything good in our lives, but Jesus wants to give us life to the full (John 10:10). Not everything bad that happens in our lives is caused by the devil, but we do need to be aware of his schemes and learn how to war against them.

Paul continues.

> Therefore take up the whole armor of God, that you may be able to withstand in the evil day, and having done all, to stand firm. Stand therefore, having fastened on the belt of truth, and having put on the breastplate of righteousness, and, as shoes for your feet, having put on the readiness given by the gospel of peace. In all circumstances take up the shield of faith, with which you can extinguish all the flaming darts of the evil one; and take the helmet of salvation, and the sword of the Spirit, which is the word of God, praying at all times in the Spirit, with all prayer and supplication. (Ephesians 6:13–18)

The only way we can win the battle against the enemy is to clothe ourselves in Jesus's armor: truth, righteousness, faith, readiness, and salvation. We also must learn how to use God's Word and prayer to murder demonic attacks.

This battleground takes place mainly in our minds. The enemy doesn't come with a pitchfork and red horns but with a thought that sounds beautiful and freeing but is contrary to what God says. Rather than entertaining these thoughts, we must learn to take them captive and make them obedient to Christ. When one of these crazy thoughts enters my mind, whether it's a thought to use drugs, demonic lust, or unbelief, I handle it in the same way. First, I pray, asking God to take this thought away and replace it with what is true. This takes care of many demonic thoughts, but if it remains, I reach out to a godly friend and expose the lie to him. I ask him to speak more truth to me and pray for me. This step is never easy because darkness hates the light. Once I have prayed to God and exposed the thought to a trusted friend, I turn my attention and thoughts to something excellent, like serving someone else or listening to a sermon or worship music.

The devil is a liar and is a pain in the you know what, but you have the power to overcome him. "He who is in you is greater than he who is in the world" (1 John 4:4). "We are more than conquerors through him who loved us" (Romans 8:37). "No weapon that is fashioned against you shall succeed" (Isaiah 54:17). The same power that raised Jesus from the dead lives inside you; therefore, you can live in victory over all demonic opposition.

Pitfall 2- Testing and Persecution

The second person in Jesus's parable is one who receives Jesus with joy at first, but once they face opposition and persecution, they fall away. The Bible is clear that following Jesus will not be easy. "In the world you will have tribulation. But take heart; I have overcome the world" (John 16:33). "Indeed, all who desire to live a godly life in Christ Jesus will be persecuted" (2 Timothy 3:12). The gospel doesn't promise an easy life, but it does promise we will have God and He will be enough regardless of our circumstances.

The next chapter will be entirely devoted to difficult seasons, so this portion will only address persecution due to your faith in Jesus. I know it's hard to believe, but not everyone will like that you are a Jesus follower. Jesus said,

> If the world hates you, know that it has hated me before it hated you. If you were of the world, the world would love you as its own; but because you are not of the world, but I chose you out of the world, therefore the world hates you. Remember the word that I said to you: "A servant is not greater than his master." If they persecuted me, they will also persecute you. (John 15:18–20)

Jesus promises all types of people will despise you because you have decided to follow Jesus.

One of my closest friends was highly involved in the secular recovery world when Jesus saved him. He had been sober for eight years, spoke to thousands of people each year about recovery, and was one of the most respected voices in the state on the topic. To everyone else, he looked like he was thriving, but on the inside, he was dying. He started rationalizing secret sin, like cheating on his wife, because he was still sober, but his soul was at complete unrest. After a series of God-ordained relationships, he turned his life over to Jesus and began pursuing full-time ministry. Much of the recovery community turned their backs on him, telling him he was going to get high because he had forgotten where he came from. The statewide recovery convention retracted their invitation for him to speak at their annual conference and he was slandered for his conversion. My friend is still a passionate follower of Jesus today, many years later, but this process was extremely painful.

I've found that not many people will criticize you for believing in "god" or becoming "spiritual," but when you begin following Jesus, you will be persecuted. In many other countries and in church history, people have even been killed for their faith in Jesus. We may not get our heads chopped off, but we should expect people to slander us and persecute us in one way or another.

One lady experienced this when she came to Jesus as He was eating at a religious leader's house. As many pious priests were having a meal around a nice table with sanitary conversation, a sinful, dirty woman emerged. The woman, who was likely a prostitute or stripper, began ugly crying on Jesus's feet. The religious men stared in utter disarray as the whore used her hair to clean his dirty feet. The host was appalled, questioned Jesus's piety, and slandered the woman.

Jesus responded with a story.

> "A certain moneylender had two debtors. One owed five hundred denarii, and the other fifty. When they could not pay, he cancelled the debt of both. Now which of them will love him more?" Simon answered, "The one, I suppose, for whom he cancelled the larger debt." And he said to him, "You have judged rightly." Then turning toward the woman he said to Simon, "Do you see this woman? I entered your house; you gave me no water for my feet, but she has wet my feet with her tears and wiped them with her hair. You gave me no kiss, but from the time I came in she has not ceased to kiss my feet. You did not anoint my head with oil, but she has anointed my feet with ointment. Therefore I tell you, her sins, which are many, are forgiven—for

she loved much. But he who is forgiven little,
loves little." (Luke 7:41–47)

The persecution you face may not only come from outside the church but also from religious people. I've observed that newly converted drug addicts who pour out their lives at the feet of Jesus in undignified worship are not always accepted by some churchgoers. Submit yourself to the authority of your local church, but be ready for persecution from religious people who don't have a story like yours. Jesus affirmed the sinful woman and rebuked the religious accuser.

Testing is coming. Hard times are on the way. Persecution from the rebellious and the religious is around the corner. When it occurs, we can either turn away from God, shaking our fists at him because our lives aren't perfect, or lean into His promises, trusting that He will sustain us through it all.

Pitfall 3- Earthly Pleasures

The last pitfall Jesus addresses has to do with "the cares and riches and pleasures of life." This is likely the most common, dangerous, and discrete pitfall of them all because the "choking" Jesus mentions isn't instant. It's a slow fade. We start out strong in our spiritual lives, bearing lots of healthy fruit, but we allow money, success, relationships, possessions, and other good things to choke out the God things. We slowly drift into loving the stuff God gives and away from loving God Himself.

John gives us clarity around what types of temptations are coming our way.

Do not love the world or the things in the world.
If anyone loves the world, the love of the Father
is not in him. For all that is in the world—**the**

CHRIS DEW ————————————————————————

> **desires of the flesh** and **the desires of the eyes**
> and **pride of life**—is not from the Father but is
> from the world. And the world is passing away
> along with its desires, but whoever does the will
> of God abides forever. (1 John 2:15–17; emphasis
> mine)

The three types of worldly temptations are the desires of the flesh, the desires of the eyes, and the pride of life. These are the three types of temptations people have struggled with since Adam and Eve in the garden. It's the same three that Jesus is tempted with in the wilderness before He began His itinerant ministry. It's the same ones you and I will face every day of our lives.

The pride of life is the desire to make a name for yourself or to make yourself the center of the universe. This is a continual fight for many who have begun to have some clean time under their belts. They get a promotion at work. They are celebrated for helping people. People begin turning to them for spiritual advice. None of these are bad things, but they become bad when we begin to love the applause and begin to forget that God is the reason for it all. When we let the thorns of pride continue to grow without humbling ourselves before God and others, it will choke out the work God is doing in our hearts. "Pride goes before destruction, and a haughty spirit before a fall" (Proverbs 16:18).

The desire of the eyes is the love of stuff. When we stop spending all our money on drugs and lawyer expenses, we sometimes begin to have the ability to own nice things. Again, there is nothing wrong with having nice things, but Jesus said "the *love* of money is the root of all kinds of evil." A great way to cut down this deadly vine is through generosity. The more you make, the more you should give away for the good of others. I'm a believer in enjoying all the benefits of being a child of God, including enjoying the good material gifts God gives you, but we cannot let these material possessions choke out the work of God in our hearts. This is a sneaky one that has turned many away from their first love. The presence of God is way better than the accumulation of wealth and possessions.

Lastly, and most importantly, the desires of the flesh. This is the desire to feel pleasure from this world. It includes drugs and alcohol but also sex and relationships. I have talked extensively about drugs and alcohol throughout the book, so I will address sex and relationships here. The AA book says "resentments are the number one offender" for relapse. I strongly disagree. In what I have seen, sex and unhealthy relationships are the number one offender! Although resentments are deadly, nothing has wreaked havoc on more babies in the faith than ungodly and unhealthy relationships. This may be the most crucial section of the entire book.

Sex is a beautiful thing, as is marriage. God designed them both, and they are some of the most amazing pleasures He has given us on this side of eternity, but they can also be very dangerous. It's like a fire in a fireplace. When kept in their proper context, they're so enjoyable, beautiful, and life-giving. But when that fire gets out of the fireplace, it is extremely destructive. The carpet catches on fire, and soon life as we know it is completely destroyed.

So what is God's design for this area of our lives? How can we keep the fire in the fireplace?

God's design for sex and marriage is for one man and one woman to be together forever. Sex is to be enjoyed in the context of marriage between one man and one woman. This is very clearly stated throughout the Bible (Genesis 2:24; Proverbs 5:15–19; Hebrews 13:4; Exodus 20:14; Ephesians 5:25; 1 Corinthians 6:18; 1 Thessalonians 4:3–4; Romans 1:26–27; etc.). Most of us need this area of our lives with all of its past perversions to be crucified and resurrected into something brand new. I don't have time to unpack all of the intricacies of this, but I would recommend a few things. First, if you are married to someone of the opposite sex, stay married, and love your spouse with Christ's love, enjoying all the sexual pleasures marriage has to offer. Next, if you are not married, don't start a relationship for at least a year. This timeline is not explicitly stated in the Bible, but I have observed that it takes at least that long for people to get their wits about them to be able to make wise lifelong decisions. Use these twelve precious months to focus solely on your relationship with Jesus. I promise you will not regret it! Lastly, once you are ready for a relationship, find someone who is also a fully devoted follower of Jesus. Many have jumped into a relationship with hopes of helping them and have found that it's much easier for them to pull you away from Christ than for you to pull them toward Him.

My wife and I met a few years after I started following Jesus and started dating a few years later. We waited until we were married to have sex, and it's been one of the best decisions of my life. God has definitely blessed our obedience. She loves Jesus and makes my life and ministry so much better! She is a tool God has used to make me more like Jesus. My life is evidence God has the power to redeem this aspect of your life too, no matter how far you have strayed. Holiness is possible in this area.

Don't Take the Bait

I have always wondered how fish can be stupid enough to sacrifice their life for a tiny piece of food. Don't they see the shiny metal thing on the string? But this is exactly what many of us do. The devil and the world work together to tempt our flesh with mouthwatering instant gratification. The bait comes in many delectable forms: the most exciting party; a rare strain of organic weed; a girl with just the right hair color, figure, smile, and personality; or a job that will make all your wildest dreams come true. Temptations have perfect timing to pop up when this whole following Jesus thing isn't going your way.

Instant gratification is alluring, but it comes with a price. The bait the devil is dangling has a hook in the middle of it. The initial taste is absolutely delicious, but it doesn't last very long because the taste of blood quickly fills your mouth as the captor pulls you in a direction you never wished to go. My plea to you is to not take the bait. No matter how tasty it looks, we must remember the hook. It will drag you out of the Living Water you love and need and into the pain and emptiness of life outside God's will.

Temptation works in a predictable progression. First comes the initial desire, which progresses to a lingering thought, which materializes into an action. First you see that piece of cake, but your willpower helps you resist. Soon you find yourself thinking about the icing and the sweet sprinkles on it. Lastly, you eventually eat the cake. This works in all areas of our lives. First you have the desire to get high again, then you dwell on it without telling anyone, and then eventually you're at the crack house. First you see an attractive person who isn't your spouse, then you begin daydreaming about how it would be to be intimate with them, and then you have the affair. Rather than allowing this progression to have its way in our lives, we must kill it before it ever becomes a reality. We must kill it at desire! When we see the enticing bait, we must pray, confess, and do whatever it takes to not take the bait. Our very lives are on the line!

Hope for the Future

Although the opposition is fierce, Jesus does not leave us without hope in the parable. "As for that in the good soil, they are those who, hearing the word, hold it fast in an honest and good heart, and bear fruit with patience." He says there is a pathway to remaining faithful and fruitful forever. To these people, He promises a life that impacts the world a hundredfold what anyone could have thought or dreamed. This is a promise God loves to make good on! Are you one of those people?

This doesn't mean you will be perfect, but it does mean you'll give Him your all and you'll be proactive in applying everything we've already discussed in this book. You will walk boldly in your identity as a child of God. You'll be saturated in Christian community as a part of a church. You'll drink deeply of Jesus every day through spiritual disciplines and an intimate relationship with God. You'll live on mission, seeking to serve others with your entire life. And you will stay vigilant against temptations. The "honest and good" heart that is required to never fall away isn't anything we can achieve on our own; it's a heart that has been truly changed by a genuine conversion. "I will give you a new heart and put a new spirit in you; I will remove from you your heart of stone and give you a heart of flesh" (Ezekiel 36:20 NIV). If you've had a genuine conversion and devote yourself to complete and radical honesty, you will experience forever freedom.

Jesus also says the person who doesn't fall away will "bear fruit with patience." Our transformation and fruitfulness will be a much slower process than we'd like. If we're going to make it to the end, we must be patient, which only comes from the Holy Spirit. It won't be easy, but the reward will be worth it!

God can and will keep you on the right path. Jude closes his epistle with "Now to him who is able to keep you from stumbling and to present you blameless before the presence of his glory with great joy" (verse 24). In Paul's letter to the Philippians, he encourages, "And I am sure of this, that he who began a good work in you will bring it to completion at the day of Jesus Christ" (1:6).

Justice Has Been Served

This question begs to be asked: "But what about when I mess up?" The reality of life is that at some point we will all fall short in one way or another. Our past will rear its ugly head and we may find ourselves back in those familiar handcuffs while sitting in a random airport. What should our response be?

The one thing that allowed me to go free from that predicament on my honeymoon wasn't that I had read my Bible that morning or that I had just gotten married or even that I was a preacher of the gospel. The one thing that allowed me to go free was the fact that justice had already been served. Those charges were null and void because many years ago my lawyer had pleaded my case to a judge who smacked the gavel and declared me to be forgiven of all my past charges, including this arrest warrant.

If you are in Christ, Jesus has pleaded your case to the judge, and He has declared you innocent. The gavel has fallen and every single charge that has come against you has been taken care of, based on what Jesus has done on your behalf. When your past rears its head or you fall short, drag your case back to the gospel! Rather than running away from God when you mess up, run to Him, knowing that it's already been paid for. Just like when those officers removed my cuffs, God will remove your chains and restore you! You are free forever because justice has already been served.

Action

1. What are some of the main lies the devil puts into your mind on a regular basis? How can you replace these with truth?

2. What will your response be when people persecute you for your faith?

3. What are the main ways you are tempted by the pleasures of the world? How will you respond when these desires come?

4. How is life going to look if you continue to stay faithful to Jesus? Spend some time journaling about the "hundredfold" life that Jesus is promising you.

CHAPTER 11

Suffering Well

Ashlyn Blocker had a normal childhood in a small Georgia town with one exception: she literally felt no pain. She has a rare genetic disease called CIPA, which stands for cognitive insensitivity to pain and anhidrosis.[32] Cuts and bruises on the playground never led to tears, and visits to the doctor for annual shots were never a burden. This may seem like a perfect scenario for a kid, but after closer investigation, it's a heartbreaking disease that's caused Ashlyn's family much distress. She's accidentally bit through her tongue, pulled the flesh off one of her fingers, and nearly always has a black eye or bruised lip. Some with this same disease have even died from their appendix bursting or internal infections that have gone untreated.[33] Pain has a purpose.

---

[32] Heidi Moawad, MD, "CIPA Disease: When a Person Can't Feel Pain," Very Well Health, reviewed April 16, 2020, https://www.verywellhealth.com/cipa-disease-when-a-person-can-t-feel-pain-4122549.
[33] "Rare Disease Makes Girl Unable to Feel Pain," Children's Health on NBC News, Associated Press, last updated November 1, 2004, http://www.nbcnews.com/id/6379795/ns/health-childrens_health/t/rare-disease-makes-girl-unable-feel-pain/#.XfE-wZNKjBJ.

Just as God set up our bodies to alert us when something harmful is happening, He's also done the same with our souls. C. S. Lewis said, "Pain insists on being attended to. God whispers to us in our pleasures, he speaks in our conscience, but he shouts in our pain. It is his megaphone to rouse a deaf world."[34] Pain is evidence something is wrong and needs to be attended to. For years we have numbed the pain in our souls with drugs and alcohol, afflicting ourselves with a spiritual form of CIPA, but now that the drugs have been removed, we must deal with these soul afflictions.

Just as physical pain is there to make us aware of something that will harm us, pain in our soul is there to make us aware of sin, which will kill us if left unnoticed. Without physical pain, we will injure our bodies, as with the latter in our souls. Just as you pull your hand back instantly from a stovetop or a fighter taps out before his opponent breaks his arm, we feel spiritual pain when we are around something contrary to God's perfection. Pain is our reaction to living in a fallen world. We were made for eternal ecstasy in perfection with God; therefore, when we encounter sin, our souls will let us know something is wrong. Some of this pain will be self-inflicted, sometimes it will be God doing surgery on our hearts to cut out what is bad, and other times, it's simply because we live in a fallen world of no fault of our own. Pain will not go away completely until we are in heaven, where sin is entirely eradicated.

The hope of this chapter isn't to explain every single bit of pain you experience but to change your perspective and help you navigate the pain, no matter what the cause is. Rather than filling our bodies with pain pills to cover the cancer that torments us, we are surrendering to the master surgeon's scalpel to get the root cause for complete healing.

---

[34] CS Lewis, *The Problem of Pain* (1940; repr.,New York, NY: HarperCollins Publishers, 2001).

Pain Is on the Way

When many first become Christians, they have the false impression that everything will now go well for them in every aspect of life. They believe all suffering will be eliminated and their lives will consist of rainbows, roses, and pots of gold. The Bible does have some promises of prosperity, but Jesus also promises we will suffer. "I have told you all this so that you may have peace in me. Here on earth you will have many trials and sorrows. But take heart, because I have overcome the world" (John 16:33 NIV). Peter echoes this. "Beloved, do not be surprised at the fiery trial when it comes upon you to test you, as though something strange were happening to you. But rejoice insofar as you share Christ's sufferings, that you may also rejoice and be glad when his glory is revealed" (1 Peter 4:12). As does Paul. "For it has been granted to you that for the sake of Christ you should not only believe in him but also suffer for his sake" (Philippians 1:29). I heard someone once say we are either in a trial, coming out of a trial, or about to go into a trial. God does not promise you an easy life on this side of eternity, but He does promise He will be with you through it all and He will be enough regardless of your circumstances.

In the previous chapters, I have addressed self-inflicted pain from personal sin that needs to be repented of, pain inflicted by others in our past where we need to extend forgiveness, demonic affliction we can cast out, and persecution due to you being a Jesus follower. In this chapter, I will focus mainly on general pain from living in a fallen world, hopefully giving you a fresh perspective on your suffering and filling you with hope to persevere. First, let's look at two types of pain.

1- Internal Pain

For the first year of sobriety, the only time I felt okay in my own skin was when I was alone with God, in church, or when I was talking about Jesus. One of my mentors used to say, "I feel like a turd in a punchbowl at a formal dinner party." This is a slightly graphic analogy, but it is a quite accurate depiction of my past internal state. The opiate withdrawals vanished after a little over a week; the benzodiazepine withdrawals remained for what seemed like months, but the awkwardness remained. If you are through with the withdrawal process, you've made it through the worst and it only gets better from here, but it's a process. Even after these initial feelings of awkwardness weaken and eventually vanish, the emotional lives of ex-addicts often take time to even out.

It feels like you are in a tiny boat in the middle of an uncontrollable sea. Some days the sea is calm, the sun is out, the temperature is just right, and extraterrestrial peace fills your soul, but other days, the hurricane seas bring confusion and even terror. Jesus's earliest followers can relate.

> Then he [Jesus] got into the boat and his disciples followed him. Suddenly a furious storm came up on the lake, so that the waves swept over the boat. But Jesus was sleeping. The disciples went and woke him, saying, "Lord, save us! We're going to drown" (Matthew 8:23–25)!

They followed Jesus right into a storm.

What happened next should encourage us. "He replied, 'You of little faith, why are you so afraid?' Then he got up and rebuked the winds and the waves, and it was completely calm" (verse 26). Over time the chemicals in your brain will balance themselves out and these highs and lows will be less intense.

Whether it be from past sin against us, lingering chemical effects from years in active addiction, or some other internal issue, we are likely to experience internal pain as we follow Jesus. It may feel like a dog fight, but as we cling to Jesus in our desperation, He promises to calm the stormy seas of our souls.

2- External Pain

You will also face seasons of external pain. I am no exception. Losing my best friend to heroin overdose, finding my dad dead of a heart attack on his bedroom floor, and hearing the news of countless friends overdosing without resuscitation have been dreadfully painful. I once went through a year of constant itching that kept me up all night, which turned out to be a severe case of eczema. One of the worst, and most sanctifying, pains I've experienced is wrestling through the progressive healing of a severe speech impediment. I'm not sure exactly what you're going through or will go through. Your list may make mine look JV, or you may be thinking, *I'm glad I'm not in his shoes.* Whatever your case may be, we need to know that on this side of eternity, we will face many trials and before they blindside us; we need to get a strong grasp on the theology of suffering. How can you persevere through these seasons? What do you do when someone breaks your heart or you lose a loved one? How should you respond when the doctor's report isn't what you hoped for? Why is there an entire chapter on pain in a book about joy? What is our hope amid these difficult times? Let's look at four benefits of trials.

1- Intimacy

One of my mentors has said, "The Christian life is a series of mountain peaks and deep valleys. The mountain peaks are where you get to see God, but the valleys are where you get to know Him." I've found this to be true throughout my Christian journey. When I am in the pit, I experience desperation for God and my intimacy with Him expands. Earthly pain is not opposed to joy in God; sometimes it's actually a catalyst for more joy in Him. The psalmist affirms this. "The Lord is near to the brokenhearted and saves the crushed in spirit" (34:18). God is drawn to suffering people. Rather than shaking your fist at Him because you're in the valley, cling to Him and enjoy the richness of His sweet presence.

One of my favorite stories in the Bible is found in Daniel 3, when three Hebrew boys get thrown in a fiery furnace because they refused to worship the golden statue set up by King Nebuchadnezzar. After heating the furnace seven times hotter and binding the three boys, the king was awestruck by what he saw.

> Then King Nebuchadnezzar was astonished and rose up in haste. He declared to his counselors, "Did we not cast three men bound into the fire?" They answered and said to the king, "True, O king." He answered and said, "But I see four men unbound, walking in the midst of the fire, and they are not hurt; and the appearance of the fourth is like a son of the gods." (verses 24–25)

They were not harmed because Jesus was in the fire with them. When you experience the fires of life, you can know that you are not alone, and Jesus is with you in the fire. You can have hope in pain because you will experience more intimacy with God as you cling to Him no matter what.

2- Growth

The other incredible thing to point out about mountaintops and valleys is not much grows on top of a mountain, but the most fertile soil is typically in the deepest valleys. God will sometimes allow pain to come into our lives to plant new things that will give us more abundant life in the future. We get a picture of this in Jesus's sermon to his disciples in John 15.

> I am the true vine, and my Father is the vinedresser.
> Every branch in me that does not bear fruit he
> takes away, and every branch that does bear fruit
> he prunes, that it may bear more fruit. (verses 1–2)

The painful process of pruning is not purposeless but will lead to "more fruit" and growth in the future.

Another great illustration I've clung to in difficult times is the purification process of silver. It was often purified by being heated by fire until the impurities would rise to the top and be removed by the silversmith. This process would be repeated until the silversmith could see his reflection in the shiny piece of metal. As the circumstances of life heat you up, God will use it to purify you and transform you into His image. Suffering is a catalyst for sanctification.

We see this in the story about the three Hebrew boys. When they were thrown into the fire, they were enslaved, but when they came out, they were free. Maybe God wants to use these hard circumstances to free you of lingering strongholds and grow you up in the faith.

3- Purpose

A close pastor friend of mine, Davey Blackburn, left his house one morning for his normal CrossFit workout. Upon returning home, he found his pregnant wife lying on the floor with a gunshot wound to the head. It was a burglary gone wrong. She was rushed to the hospital and eventually passed away from the trauma.

Davey was distraught. Most people would use this as a reason to turn away from God, shaking their fist at heaven and wondering how God could let this happen, but Davey reacted differently. After many weeks and months of confusion, wrestling, and leaning into God for comfort, he felt compelled to use his pain to comfort others. Davey started a podcast that now reaches tens of thousands of people, wrote a book, and travels the world helping people find purpose in their pain. He has come to believe that nothing is wasted.

Paul encourages us to do the same.

> Blessed be the God and Father of our Lord Jesus Christ, the Father of mercies and God of all comfort, who comforts us in all our affliction, so that we may be able to comfort those who are in any affliction, with the comfort with which we ourselves are comforted by God. For as we share abundantly in Christ's sufferings, so through Christ we share abundantly in comfort too. (2 Corinthians 1:3–5)

God is the master of taking awful circumstances and using them to help others. When the three Hebrews boys came out of the fire, King Nebuchadnezzar made a decree that the whole country would only worship the Hebrew boys' God. God used a fiery trial to reach an entire nation.

Whatever your pain, God can use it to help others. Just as my past addiction is helping people recover and Davey's loss is comforting thousands, your pain can have purpose too. Rather than playing the victim role, you can echo Joseph's reaction to extreme pain. "As for you, you meant evil against me, but God meant it for good, to bring it about that many people should be kept alive, as they are today" (Genesis 50:20).

4- Eternal Life

Maybe the most encouraging thing to focus on amid pain and suffering is the reality of eternal life. "For I consider that the sufferings of this present time are not worth comparing with the glory that is to be revealed to us" (Romans 8:18). One fragment of a second in the presence of God is going to be worth decades of intense suffering. The sublime joy of heaven and life on the new earth is going to make every moment of suffering worth it.

We get a picture of what this will be like.

> He will wipe away every tear from their eyes, and death shall be no more, neither shall there be mourning, nor crying, nor pain anymore, for the former things have passed away. And he who was seated on the throne said, "Behold, I am making all things new." (Revelation 21:4–5)

John goes into greater detail to show the

> river of the water of life, bright as crystal, flowing from the throne of God and of the Lamb through the middle of the street of the city; also, on either side of the river, the tree of life with its twelve kinds of fruit, yielding its fruit each month. The leaves of the tree were for the healing of the nations. No longer will there be anything accursed, but the throne of God and of the Lamb will be in it, and his servants will worship him. They will see his face, and his name will be on their foreheads. And night will be no more. They will need no light of lamp or sun, for the Lord God will be their light, and they will reign forever and ever. (22:1–5)

There is coming a day when all sin, pain, and sadness will be wiped away completely. Currently,

> we don't yet see things clearly. We're squinting in a fog, peering through a mist. But it won't be

> long before the weather clears and the sun shines bright! We'll see it all then, see it all as clearly as God sees us, knowing him directly just as he knows us! (1 Corinthians 13:12 MSG)

If you are in Christ, you will live immersed in full intimacy with God for eternity. Fullness of joy and pleasures forevermore will be your reality forever. Because of this truth, we can have hope in the face of earthly suffering.

Our Example

The ultimate example of how to suffer well is Jesus. He was falsely accused, arrested, spit on, beaten, and eventually nailed to a piece of wood and brutally murdered. Knowing this was coming, he prayed, "My Father, if it be possible, let this cup pass from me; nevertheless, not as I will, but as you will" (Matthew 26:39). Just like you and me, Jesus didn't want to suffer, but He submitted to the Father's will, trusting He knows best. We can trust the Father even when we'd rather take the easier route.

Imagine if you'd never seen *Star Wars* before but walked in a theater that was showing one of the nine marathon movies. You watched about twenty seconds and then wrote George Lucas a letter explaining all of the things that are wrong with the story line. This is exactly what we do with God. Rather than trusting His eternal perspective, we criticize what we see unfolding. Romans 8:28 promises, "And we know that for those who love God all things work together for good, for those who are called according to his purpose." No matter what is going on in your life right now, you can trust that God is working it together for your good if you love Him and are living for Him. He is the best director, and His story line is playing out perfectly. Spoiler alert: if you are in Christ, there is a happy ending!

Count It All Joy

The author of Hebrews gives us some more insight on how Jesus was able to endure. "For the joy that was set before him endured the cross, despising the shame, and is seated at the right hand of the throne of God" (Hebrews 12:2). Jesus was able to suffer well because of the inexpressible joy that was in the future.

James encourages us to join Jesus in having this mind-set toward suffering.

> Count it all joy, my brothers, when you meet trials of various kinds, for you know that the testing of your faith produces steadfastness. And let steadfastness have its full effect, that you may be perfect and complete, lacking in nothing. (James 1:2–4)

Pain is a means to more joy because through it, your faith and endurance are strengthened. It won't be easy in the moment, but it is worth it!

One of the most realistic pictures of what this looks like is a scene from the movie *Shawshank Redemption*.[35] Andy Dufresne was falsely accused of murdering his wife and was serving a life sentence in Shawshank Prison. After many years of being beaten, raped, and mistreated, he'd had enough. He began to use a tiny pickaxe to chisel through the prison wall. Over the course of many years, he finally reached a sewage pipe. In the middle of one stormy night, as thunder cracks filled the prison, he climbed through the wall, used a sharp rock to punch a hole in the sewage pipe, and squeezed inside the foulest place anyone has ever been. He barely fit like a man in a straitjacket. Throughout the night, he

---

[35] *Shawshank Redemption*, directed by Frank Darabont, Columbia Pictures, 1994.

crawled through five hundred yards of inmate excrement, puking every few feet.

After hours of trudging through the disgusting sewage, he reached the end. He fell out of the end of the pipe into a river. Freedom! As the pouring rain washed him clean, he looked up into the sky with his hands raised in complete ecstasy. It was worth it.

The Choice

When you face hard times, both internally and externally, you have a choice. You can either run back to the needle, bottle, or pipe to numb your pain for a minute or you can fight to keep your eyes on Jesus. Running to your old lover will satisfy for a moment but end in more pain and destruction. Running to God will increase your intimacy, grow you spiritually, give you massive purpose, and fill you with hope for everlasting joy. Following Jesus is not easy, but it's worth it.

Action

1. What are the hardest things happening in your life right now, both internally and externally? How are you currently dealing with these pain points?
2. Based on what we've discussed, how can you cultivate more intimacy with Jesus during hard times?
3. How could you use your pain to help someone else today or in the near future?
4. Is there anything in your life where you are not following God's will because you think you know better? How can you surrender that to Him today?

CHAPTER 12

Leaving a Legacy of Joy

One of the stories in the Bible I can relate with most is found in Luke 8, when Jesus meets a man oppressed by a legion of demons. This man was like the town junkie. He roamed the streets, bringing chaos wherever he went. The police officers arrested him often, but the chains couldn't restrain him. He ran around naked, cutting himself with rocks and driving the townspeople crazy. Not having anywhere to live, he slept in tombs away from civilization. Rather than avoiding him, Jesus intentionally went out of his way to meet him. When the demonized man saw Jesus, he fell down, begging Jesus not to torment him. Jesus cast the demons out of the man, and he was healed. When the townspeople came out to see what had happened, they found the previously possessed man "sitting at the feet of Jesus, clothed, and in his right mind" (Luke 8:35).

This is a picture of what happened to me and what I pray has likely happened to you. Before I met Jesus, I was enslaved to the demonic forces of addiction. The city I lived in rightfully viewed me as a menace to society and consistently tried to restrain the chaos. I was a mess until Jesus went out of His way to save me, heal me, and set me free. If you have read this far and have taken the action steps after each chapter, you can probably relate. You are no longer the menace you once were. Jesus has set you free! You are sitting at the feet of Jesus in your right mind.

The word Luke uses to describe the state of the man after his encounter with Jesus comes from the Greek word *sozo*. This word is often translated "saved," but it means much more than making you positionally right with God. It also means healed, delivered, and rescued. When it says this man was healed, it means Jesus saved his soul, cast out the demons that tormented him, and delivered him into the safety of God's protection. Jesus has given you access to this same sozo. "By His wounds we are healed" (Isaiah 53:5 NIV).

After seeing the state of the previously possessed man, the people were filled with fear and begged Jesus to leave. As Jesus was getting into his boat, the newly saved man begged to join Him. Jesus denied his request and said, "Return to your home, and declare how much God has done for you" (verse 39). He listened and "went away proclaiming throughout the whole city how much Jesus had done for him." Historians have hypothesized that this man went on to flip his city upside down for the gospel and leave a legacy of freedom and joy in Jesus for generations to come. Like many other people throughout history, "through his faith, though he died, he still speaks" (Hebrews 11:4).

What Will Your Life Mean?

Since I met Christ, I have thought a lot about what my life will mean. As I've attended more funerals, I've heard many speeches and gazed at many tombstones. I've sometimes wondered, *What will people say at my funeral? What difference will I make? What will the dash between my birth date and death date represent?*

What will my life speak when I'm not here anymore? What will change in eternity because of my life? What legacy will I leave?

For many people with pasts like you and me, the answer to that question is to stay sober. They think, *If I can live the rest of my life without using drugs, I will have fulfilled my purpose.* This is definitely a noble cause worth shooting for, but I believe God has more in store. Jesus didn't just tell the demoniac to attempt not be possessed by demons anymore but told him to spend the rest of his life making an eternal impact and leaving a legacy. Jesus's words are still speaking to you. "Return to your home, and declare how much God has done for you." Devote the rest of your life to leaving something that will outlive your life and will matter in eternity. Your remaining years are exploding with kingdom potential.

The purpose of this chapter is to encourage you to get a vision for your life that far exceeds just staying sober. The author of Proverbs wrote, "Where there is no vision, the people perish" (29:18 KJV). I believe many people are not experiencing the abundant life Jesus promised because they have not taken the time to consider the aim of their lives. The inverse of this is also true. As you get a vision from God for your life, you will experience more life and joy than you ever thought possible. You have the potential to leave a legacy of joy in God, both in your family and all over the world.

Legacy Inside the Home

As far back as we can tell, my family has been pretty broken and practically pagan. The men in my family have often overworked while punting on many responsibilities at home. They have put the lion's share of their time and creative energies in projects outside the home, leaving their wives and kids to figure out life without a present father. They have not been men of God but men of money, position, and hard work. This has led to a wreckage of health problems, failed marriages, and substance abuse. I definitely inherited these natural inclinations, and if it wasn't for Jesus, I'd still be walking in their footsteps.

One of the most impactful conversations of my life was when my older cousin, David, who is one of the only believers in my family, helped me to reflect on my family's past. With tears in his eyes and joy in his heart, he said, "What God has done in you is the linchpin of our family story. Jesus is using you to change the direction and legacy of our family." These words have resonated with me and I pray they fill you with hope for your family too. What if you are the linchpin to change your family legacy forever? What if you are the difference maker in your family?

Chances are you come from a family like mine, to varying degrees. Whether you look back and see generations of pain, hurt, and godlessness or you come from a family of rich spiritual heritage and intense blessing, you have a role to play. All through the Bible and history, we see the reality of generational sin or blessing. Adam began the original generational curse during the Fall that he passed down to his son Cain, who became a murderer. This family curse led to mass spreading of sin and eventual destruction. Abraham, on the other hand, had a radical encounter with God, which led to genuine godly devotion that was passed down to Isaac, Jacob, Joseph, and many more. Abraham's family definitely fell short in many areas and has had some weak links in the chain, but he left a legacy of faith. We even see this in the New Testament when Paul tells Timothy, "I am reminded of your sincere faith, a faith that dwelt first in your grandmother Lois and your mother Eunice and now, I am sure, dwells in you as well" (2 Timothy 1:5). Every generation must decide for themselves if they will follow Christ or not, but parents and grandparents have great influence on that eternity-deciding decision and the type of legacy their family leaves behind.

When you became a Christian, Jesus broke the power of sin and death over your life. If you would've stayed in your addiction and sin rather than following Christ, chances are that your children and grandchildren would follow your example. But now, since Christ has raised you from the dead and healed you, you have the power to leave a legacy of blessing for many generations to come. How can we do this?

If you are married, devote yourself to loving your spouse like Christ loved the church rather than caving to the generational sin of divorce that is so prevalent in our day. If you have kids, do everything in your power to train them up in the faith. Pray with them. Read the Bible together. Sit around the table together, eating good food, sharing God's story, and casting a vision for the future of your family. Love them with Christ's love. Pray for them daily, and shoot them into the world as flaming arrows ready to make a multiplying gospel impact in this world. Live with your great-grandkids in mind.

You may be looking back at your life, discouraged at how addiction has robbed your family to this point. Maybe you've had many broken marriages or your kids have already followed in your addicted footsteps. If you are in Christ, you are completely forgiven of these shortcomings. My advice is to spend your remaining years passionately following Jesus and doing the best you can to reconcile with your kids. God promises to "restore the years the locusts have eaten." It's not too late to change the story you leave behind. Even if you are on your deathbed, you can be like the thief who was crucified next to Jesus. In his dying breath, he repented, crying out to Jesus, "Jesus, remember me when You come into Your kingdom!" And Jesus said to him, "Truly I tell you, today you will be with Me in Paradise" (Luke 23:42–43). Millions of people have been impacted by this story. This man's legacy was changed in an instant. It's not too late for you.

No matter what your family looks like up to this point, God's plan for you is to leave an impact in your family for many generations to come. His desire is for you to have a peaceful, purpose-filled house filled with His presence that leaves a lasting legacy. Your faith can still speak in your family legacy but also throughout the entire world.

Outside the Home

Jackie Pullinger is a prime example of leaving a legacy outside the home. After feeling called to be a missionary but being rejected by every missions organization, she got on a boat headed to Asia. At each port, she asked God, "Is this where You're calling me?" After dozens of stops, they finally arrived in Hong Kong and she felt the confirmation from God to get off the boat. With only a few dollars in her pocket, she got a job and moved into the most disgusting slum in all of China. This walled city was home to many Triad gang members and was consumed with opium dens and child prostitution. There was no sewage system so the residents threw their feces out windows and into streets. For years, she lived in this pigpen while sharing the gospel without seeing anyone converted, but eventually the Holy Spirit began moving in powerful ways. Heroin and opium addicts began coming to Christ by the masses. Now in her mid-seventies, God has used Jackie to lead thousands of wild people to Christ, set up dozens of rehabilitation homes, and inspired millions with her story.[36]

Jackie is leaving a lasting legacy by laying down her life for the sake of Christ. She has been willing to sacrifice lots of earthly comforts in order to live in light of eternity. Jesus emphasized this.

> Do not lay up for yourselves treasures on earth,
> where moth and rust destroy and where thieves
> break in and steal, but lay up for yourselves
> treasures in heaven, where neither moth nor rust

---

[36] Andrew Quicke and Jackie Pullinger, *Chasing the Dragon: One Woman's Struggle Against the Darkness of Hong Kong's Drug Dens* (Bloomington, MN: Chosen Books, 1980).

> destroys and where thieves do not break in and
> steal. For where your treasure is, there your heart
> will be also. (Matthew 6:19–21)

Jesus is letting us know the best way to leave a legacy is to live in light of eternity. Rather than spending our time trying to make lots of money, have lots of possessions, or even make a name for ourselves, we should pour out our lives for the glory of God and the eternal good of others.

Unless you become president or an elite athlete, chances are in a couple of generations not many people will know your name. The only thing that will matter is what you did for Christ's name. Our legacy is not for our fame but Jesus's. We should have the same posture as Isaiah, who said, "Your name and remembrance are the desire of our soul" (26:8). Or as the great reformer Count von Zinzendorf, who said, "Preach the Gospel, die, and be forgotten." For some, this may seem like joyless duty, but John Piper has noted our greatest joy is found in making God as famous as possible.[37] This is the essence of leaving a legacy of joy.

You may not be called to move to Hong Kong to live your life among opium dealers and prostitutes, but you do have a role to play. For some, this may look like moving to another country to preach the gospel, but for others, it may look like living on mission in your neighborhood. You may be called to open a treatment facility, or you may be called to serve in your local church. Whatever life God calls you to, do it to the glory of God, trusting that anything done in the Lord is not in vain. A pastor once said, "If the size of your vision for your life isn't intimidating to you, there's a good chance it's insulting to God."[38]

What is God calling you to do?

---

[37] John Piper, *Desiring God: Meditations of a Christian Hedonist* (Colorado Springs, CO: Multnomah Books, 1981).

[38] Steven Furtick, *Sun Stand Still: What Happens When You Date to Ask God for the Impossible* (Colorado Springs, CO: Multnomah Books, 2010). 7

Legacy of Joy

God wants more for your life than for you to just make it to the grave without getting high again. He wants you to join Him in changing the world and leaving a legacy of joy in Jesus. This starts in your family but then bleeds into every aspect of your life and might even impact the entire world. Paul encourages us to no longer look back at our past but focus our attention forward.

> But one thing I do: forgetting what lies behind and straining forward to what lies ahead, I press on toward the goal for the prize of the upward call of God in Christ Jesus. (Philippians 3:13–14)

He has saved you, set you free, and satisfied your soul and is now sending you on mission to live a life that makes an eternal difference.

The End

This book started with a picture of the chaos of addiction. Desperately empty, we were wasting our lives trying to find something to fill the void in our souls, leaving a wake of pain and hurt in our path. We spent our lives "rinsing cottons" and shooting up warm water to fill the void in our souls and soothe the withdrawals. We tried all the leading treatment methods but still returned to our vomit. Death, jail, or homelessness seemed our only options. All of this persisted until Jesus saved us.

The knock at the door finally came.

We heard the gospel and opened the doors of our hearts to find the One we've been waiting for. Jesus has come in our hearts and has given us the joy we were dying for. Not only has He saved our souls, but He's also satisfied our deepest longings. Through

Jesus's life, death, and resurrection, we have been made into new creations. We are no longer playing with mud pies in a slum but are able to enjoy the holiday at sea.

Life has its flavor back. Relationships are being restored. Our shame is gone. The restlessness in our souls has been replaced with a deep, abiding peace. Life is by no means easy, but we have unshakable hope and inexpressible joy. Our purposeless existence is now exploding with kingdom purpose.

Addiction has been eradicated.

We have been reconciled to God to experience endless inexpressible joy.

Jesus is the answer to addiction.

Action

1. If you have yet to turn your entire life over to Christ, do it now. Get on your knees and genuinely repent, turning everything over to Him.
2. Spend some time dreaming about what you want your life to mean. What is God saying? Write it down, and put it somewhere you can see it.
3. Thank God for saving you, setting you free, and satisfying your soul. Ask Him to use your life for His glory and your joy.

Get Off the Treadmill: Why the Twelve Steps Are Incomplete

One of the leading methods of recovery over the last hundred years has been the twelve steps of Alcoholics Anonymous (AA). There are twelve-step groups all over the world for different drugs of choice, including Narcotics Anonymous (NA), Cocaine Anonymous (CA), and even Heroin Anonymous (HA). Alcoholics Anonymous started in the 1930s when the founder, Bill Wilson, had a spiritual experience that removed the desire to drink and he began living according to the principles of the Oxford Group. This was a Christian group aimed at leading people into a relationship with God and living a godly life. The twelve steps evolved from biblical principles but have allowed room for people to come up with their own conception of God. Although the twelve steps have helped multitudes of people relieve their desire to drink, they are incomplete in many ways. In this short appendix, I will address four of those shortcomings.

1- Eternity

One of the main shortcomings of the twelve steps is the longevity of the solution. The aim of the twelve steps is to help people stop drinking and have a more fulfilled life on earth, without any consideration of what happens when we die. This is like if you came to me with a gunshot wound and I gave you a handful of OxyContin and a Band-Aid. It may relieve the pain temporarily and cover the bloody wound, but it does not help you solve the real problem.

We will all spend eternity in either heaven or hell. The emptiness in our souls that led us to alcoholism and drug addiction is meant to lead us back to God through Christ, which results in eternal life. If we rid ourselves of the temporary problem of addiction without fixing our eternal problem, we have just put a Band-Aid on a bullet wound. C. S. Lewis said, "Aim for heaven and get earth thrown in; aim for earth and get neither."[39] The principles found in the Bible lead to more than sobriety on earth. Through scripture, we can know the God of the Bible, live a godly life, and experience the joy He offers now and for eternity.

2- Grace

One of the walls I often run into with sharing Jesus with people in twelve-step recovery is the idea of religion. This stems from a fundamental misunderstanding of religion. Religion, at its core, is human's approach to God. It is the belief that we can earn our way back to God. This is at the root of every single world religion other than Christianity. Muslims, Hindus, Buddhists, and even many Catholics have this mentality. Because God is holy and we are flawed, they believe we must climb the ladder of good works and religious duty to earn our way to right relationship with God.

Christianity stands in stark opposition to this. The Bible teaches that we are unable to earn God's approval through our good works and able only through the grace of God. God doesn't

---

[39] CS Lewis, *The Joyful Christian: 127 Readings* (1984; repr., New York, NY: Touchstone, 1996), 138.

wait for you to climb the steps of religion, but He came to earth, lived a perfect life in your place, and took your punishment upon Himself on the cross. "For by grace you have been saved through faith. And this is not your own doing; it is the gift of God, not a result of works, so that no one may boast" (Ephesians 2:8–9).

Without the grace of God, the twelve steps are just another form of religion. They teach the way to unblock ourselves from God is by human steps. In other words, the twelve-step model teaches we must climb the ladder back to God through good works. This is like a man tirelessly running on a treadmill. He believes if he jumps off, he will surely drink again. The treadmill continues to speed up until the man is gasping for air. The twelve steps without the grace of God teaches that to stay right with God, you must run harder and faster for the rest of your life. Many have lasted many years in this constant striving, but Jesus invites you to get off the treadmill.

> Are you tired? Worn out? Burned out on religion? Come to me. Get away with me and you'll recover your life. I'll show you how to take a real rest. Walk with me and work with me—watch how I do it. Learn the unforced rhythms of grace. I won't lay anything heavy or ill-fitting on you. Keep company with me and you'll learn to live freely and lightly. (Matthew 11:28–30 MSG)

God does not just want you to live a godly life; He wants you to live a life of soul rest in His grace. When you place your faith in Christ, you can get off the treadmill.

3- Identity

AA teaches its members that once you are an alcoholic or addict, you remain in this state forever. Whenever a member speaks at a meeting, they open with something like "Hi, I'm Chris, and I am an alcoholic." They find their identity in their deficiency in order to remind themselves they can never drink or use again. But ironically, identifying with the past keeps them enslaved.

The Bible teaches that once you place your faith in Christ, you are a new creation. This means that all of the old labels you used to carry around have been replaced with all that Christ has bought for you. After giving a list of sinful identities, including drunkard, Paul says, "And such *were* some of you. But you were washed, you were sanctified, you were justified in the name of the Lord Jesus Christ and by the Spirit of our God" (1 Corinthians 6:11). The spiritual principles of AA may be able to change your outward actions, but the gospel changes the very core of who you are. You and I can now boldly say, "Hi, my name is Chris, and I am a new creation."

4- Idolatry

Lastly, and most importantly, the twelve steps fall short of the main issue of life: who is my god? The point of life is to know God. The point of the gospel is to get God. The problem with the world is that we look to things other than God to be our god, and they always fall short. Without a relationship with God through the gospel, we have just made something else our god (principles, group, program, etc.) that still won't satisfy the deepest longings of our soul. The crux of the issue with the twelve steps is that they allow you to pick a god of your understanding. We want god on our terms, which is the problem with all addiction and sin. God will not allow for this. God is God, and He doesn't conform to our understanding.

The point of the biblical principles of the twelve steps is to lead us into a more intimate relationship with God. Without Him, the principles are just like learning principles for a healthy marriage but having no spouse. It's like learning how to swim with no pool. We are practicing the principles yet missing the person who is the point. We have traded one false god—drugs and alcohol—for another false god: sobriety and the program of AA. We aren't emancipated from our jail cell but moved from one jail to another one in a different county. The cuffs still haven't come off.

There is one true God. Jesus said, "I am the way, and the truth, and the life. No one comes to the Father except through me" (John 14:6). A god of your own understanding or higher power may give you the power to stay sober, but there is one God who you were made to be in relationship with. He is the holiday at sea you have been longing for.

In conclusion, the twelve steps have merit in the sense that their source is the Bible, but they fall short in many devastating ways—mainly eternity, grace, identity, and idolatry. I have heard many twelve-step advocates say, "Religion [lumping Christianity into this category] is for people who don't want to go to hell. Spirituality [meaning twelve-step programs] is for people who have already been there." I will close by adding one more line to this equation.

> Religion is for people who don't want to go to hell.
> Spirituality is for people who have already been there.
> Christianity is for people who are never going back.

A Note to Loved Ones

After preaching at a church in North Carolina, an elderly couple came up to me while crying their eyes out. The lady had the most genuine and hopeless look on her face as she described their precious grandson's story. He was addicted to opioids and had robbed nearly everyone in his family multiple times. He was not interested in getting sober or coming to church. She gracefully shared that my story reminded her of their grandson and humbly asked me if I had any advice for them on how to help him.

This is definitely the question I get asked the most as I travel around the country. "How can I help my son?" "Can you help my brother?" "What should I do with my friend who is addicted?" The truth is there is no pill we can give them that will heal their drug addiction, but there are principles that will help.

Advice 1- Keep the Relationship Intact, but Don't Enable

For some parents and friends, their natural bent is to completely cut ties with the person in addiction. They view addiction as a pure choice that the person is making and treat them with anger and contempt rather than love. For others, their natural bent is to just "love" the addict. This type of person does everything they can to support their child or friend, not knowing that they are enabling them and doing more damage than help.

As we look at how Jesus dealt with alcoholics, tax collectors, sinners, prostitutes, and strippers in the Bible, we see that He modeled for us how to manage this delicate tension. Jesus spent time with people who were active in sin, so much so that the religious elite of His day condemned him guilty by association. We also see that Jesus's definition of love was not to enable the person to do whatever they want. In John 8, after showing a woman caught in adultery incredible grace, Jesus tells the woman, "I don't condemn you; go, and from now on sin no more."

My plea to you is to keep the relationship intact with the person struggling with addiction, but don't enable them. Take them out to dinner for a meaningful conversation and some good laughs, but don't give them money. Have them over for dinner, but don't pay their bills. Love them, but don't "love" them to death.

Advice 2- Pray for Them and Care for Them Spiritually

I am sure that one of the main reasons I'm alive today is due to the prayers of some close friends and family members who would not give up on me. While there are many contributing factors to addiction, in my experience, the epidemic of addiction is mainly spiritual in nature. That means the solution is also mainly spiritual. In Luke 18, Jesus tells the parable of the persistent widow. The widow asks the judge so many times that he finally caves to the devoted lady's request. Jesus's point of the parable is that we should pray without giving up or losing heart. Your prayers have the potential to completely change things.

We also know that faith without works is dead. In Mark 2, four friends were willing to do whatever it took to get their paralytic friend to Jesus. They didn't just pray for healing; they also carried him many miles and then cut a hole in the roof of the place Jesus was preaching. The Bible says "because of their faith" he was healed. This does not mean shoving condemning scripture down the addict's throat, but it does mean loving them well, letting your conversations be filled with grace and seasoned with salt, and bringing them to places to have an encounter with Jesus. What if God used you to play a part in Him saving your friend or family member?

Advice 3- Don't Make Them the Center of Your Universe

One of the biggest issues I see and hear about among people close to drug addicts, especially parents, is that their lives become centered around the addict. They put more focus on their child than on their marriage or anything else that used to be important in their lives. When parents do this, it is not helping the problem but making it worse.

Don't put the addict above your own marriage, and definitely don't let them become the center of your life. The only way that you are going to be of any help to your hurting friend or family member is if Jesus is at the center of your universe, where He belongs. When we center our lives around anything other than God, our lives begin to crumble. When your life is centered on Christ and you have a strong marriage, you will be much more helpful to your hurting loved one.

I want to plead with you not to try to become a practical savior to your loved one. You are not powerful enough to save them. What happens to them is not your fault either way. Your main role is to love them and pray for them, but don't allow their addiction to become the focal point of your life.

Lastly, I want to encourage you that there is hope. I have seen hundreds of drug addicts meet Christ and learn to live in true freedom and real joy, including the grandson of the couple I mentioned at the beginning of this appendix. My family and friends had all but given up on me after many rehabs and broken promises, but God did a miracle. Love them like Jesus does, pray for them, and make Jesus the center of your universe!

APPENDIX 3

A Note to Pastors

I have done my best in this short book to explain why the real answer to addiction is Jesus Christ. As you have read, addiction is a very complex issue that involves the mind, will, emotions, body, soul, and spirit. Many of the current methods of treatment focus on one or two of these aspects and add value in the fight against the addiction epidemic but do not get to the root. If the real answer to addiction is spiritual, mainly a Jesus answer, there are massive implications for pastors. We have a major role in battling this epidemic. We cannot punt on this anymore, claiming that the rehabs, counselors, and other medical professionals will solve it. These are all useful tools, but it is the church's job to bring the transforming joy of God to the godless. It's our job to bring the gospel, and the freedom available in Christ, to drug addicts.

If you are a pastor who's made it this far in the book, thank you for leaning in and giving many hours to learning about addiction. Many pastors I talk to about this issue have a heart to help but don't know where to start. They feel powerless. If you can relate, this appendix is for you. You may have family members and friends who are battling addiction. You may have people in your church and ministry who have lost loved ones to this dreadful darkness. You may even have people in your church who can't seem to break free themselves. Addiction is everywhere, and we have the antidote.

The next few pages will not answer all your questions or give you a foolproof plan on reaching every addict in your city, but they will give you a good place to start. I am going to offer three reasons why I believe every pastor should make it their aim to reach the addicts in their city and then three practical steps that will get you started.

Why Should You Focus on Helping the Addiction Epidemic?

1. Jesus modeled going after addicts.

Although the term *addict* is not explicitly stated in the Bible, Jesus clearly modeled going after the people who were menaces to society. The clearest example is the demoniac we discussed in chapter 12. Jesus intentionally went out of his way to meet this man who was enslaved by the influence of demonic forces that caused him to hurt himself and others around him. In Mark 2:17, Jesus said, "Those who are well have no need of a physician, but those who are sick. I came not to call the righteous, but the sinners." Jesus didn't just come for the "almost saved" but the desperately wicked.

The story of the prodigal son in Luke 15 is Jesus's response to the Pharisees' grumbling about Jesus spending too much time with the tax collectors and sinners.

> Now the tax collectors and sinners were all drawing near to hear him. And the Pharisees and the scribes grumbled, saying, "This man receives sinners and eats with them." (verses 1–2)

What if the other churches in your area grumbled about the sinfulness of who attends your church?

We even see prophecies about Jesus's focus on the "wild beasts" in the Old Testament.

> I will make a way in the wilderness and rivers in the desert. The wild beasts will honor me, the jackals and the ostriches, for I give water in the wilderness, rivers in the desert, to give drink to my chosen people. (Isaiah 43:19-20)

Jesus's ministry is summed up with simplicity in Luke 19:10, which says, "The Son of Man came to seek and to save the lost." We see this play out in John 4 with the woman at the well, in John 8 with the woman caught in adultery, and dozens of other places in the gospels.

Jesus clearly modeled going after the worst of sinners, especially the people society had written off as hopeless. Drug addicts definitely fall in this category.

2. Jesus commanded us to go after addicts.

Not only did Jesus model going after people like drug addicts with the gospel, but He also commanded it. We obviously know the Great Commission in Matthew 28:19, "Therefore, go and make disciples of all nations," and in Mark 16:15, "Go into all the world and preach the Gospel to the whole creation." But another command that specifies the type of people we should go after is found in Luke 14:21. "Go out quickly to the streets and lanes of the city and bring in the poor and crippled and blind and lame." And then Luke 14 says, "Go out to the highways and hedges and compel people to come in that my house may be filled" (verse 23). Jesus is telling us to bring the gospel *into the wild* so the *wild beasts* may be saved, set free, and sent on mission by Jesus Christ. William

Booth summed up Jesus's life and command excellently when he said, "Go straight for souls and go for the worst." Let's take Jesus's example and commands seriously by devoting our lives to preaching the gospel and making disciples, especially going to the "worst" of souls, such as drug addicts.

3. There is no greater tool to advance the kingdom than an addict set free.

Not only is it biblical to reach drug addicts with the gospel, but it is also strategically wise for your church. Yes, reaching drug addicts is messy and oftentimes heartbreaking, but it is my experience and observation that there is no greater tool to advance God's kingdom on earth than an addict set free!

They will not be the most generous financial givers and they will take more pastoral care time than many of your other church members, but with regard to passion, worship, and evangelism, there is no comparison. If you want to infuse fresh zeal for God and His mission into your church, go after drug addicts. If you want to awaken your people to what it looks like to worship like Mary, rather than Martha, go after drug addicts. I've heard many pastors say, after they've experienced a couple of these stories, they'd rather have ten ex-addicts in their church than 1,000 regular church attendees.

In the post-truth and post-Christian world we live in, people may argue with you over the infallibility of the Bible and other doctrines, but they cannot argue an addict set free. What if addicts being set free is one of the tools God is going to use to soften the hearts of the world to the reality of Jesus and the transforming power of the gospel?

Let's not try to tame these wild ones, but let's unleash them to live in wild worship and on wild mission for the kingdom of God. Let them make your congregation feel uncomfortable by their passionate, undignified worship. Let them wear whatever clothes they wish. Encourage them to invite their drug addict friends to church. This type of ministry is not another charity to throw money at but a missionary training ground to invest in. The long-term fruit is well worth the investment and "sacrifice" it will require.

Where should you start?

1. Pray and ask God what your area of investment and impact will be.

I do not want you to jump into something God isn't calling you to, so let's begin in prayer. Spend some time on your knees asking God what He's specifically calling you to. Maybe it's just a small tweak in mission to begin reaching more drug addicts, or maybe it's a complete overhaul. Ask Him, "In light of what I've read in this book, what are You saying to me? What part should our church play in pushing back this darkness?"

2. Begin meeting with people in your church and community who've overcome addiction.

A good starting place is to begin meeting with people in your community who have experience in the addiction lifestyle and have overcome it. Ask them lots of questions to learn as much about their story and the needs of the community as possible. Ask them to get involved and help lead the way. Rather than trying to do it yourself, make it your aim to empower experienced people. You by no means have to have a past in addiction to reach addicts, but it certainly helps to have some people who do on the team. If you don't know anyone like this, start investing in one person who's still in addiction. It's amazing how a personal relationship with an addict will teach you about addiction and break your heart for people struggling with it.

3. Do something.

Whether it's starting Celebrate Recovery, creating your own program, or using this book and subsequent small group content, just start somewhere. Whether it's going to the methadone clinic to hand out food and invite cards to your church or partnering with a treatment center and finding a way for them to attend your church, just start somewhere. Whether it's starting a prison ministry or an open share meeting, just start somewhere. Chances are you won't solve the addiction epidemic in your city by yourself, but you can play a part. I believe God will give you a vision for what this may look like.

One church in Bradenton, Florida, where heroin addiction is rampant, has gained the reputation of the heroin church. They haven't reached many people personally struggling with addiction but felt called to begin fostering the children impacted by their parents' addiction. Dozens of kids have now found healthy homes in their church family! This is a beautiful example of asking God for your church's niche and then just starting somewhere. What could this look like for your church?

The real answer to addiction is Jesus Christ. The main answer is not politics, psychology, or criminal justice reform. The answer is the church! What might it look like if thousands of pastors all over the world took Jesus at His Word and began reaching and discipling people in addiction? What might it look like for tens of thousands of drug addicts to be saved, set free, and sent on mission? How might the world be flipped upside down for the gospel? Could it be the next wave of revival in our world?

ABOUT THE AUTHOR

Chris Dew is a traveling evangelist and author based out of Anderson, South Carolina. He is married to his beautiful wife, Kathleen.